Campus with Purpose

Campus with Purpose

~

Building a Mission-Driven Campus

STEPHEN LEHMKUHLE

Rutgers University Press

New Brunswick, Camden, and Newark, New Jersey, and London

Library of Congress Cataloging-in-Publication Data
Names: Lehmkuhle, Stephen W., 1951– author.
Title: Campus with purpose : building a mission-driven campus /
Stephen Lehmkuhle.
Description: New Brunswick, New Jersey : Rutgers University Press, 2020. |
Includes bibliographical references and index.
Identifiers: LCCN 2020004898 | ISBN 9781978818361 (paperback) |
ISBN 9781978818378 (hardcover) | ISBN 9781978818385 (epub) |
ISBN 9781978818392 (mobi) | ISBN 9781978818408 (pdf)
Subjects: LCSH: University of Minnesota, Rochester—Planning. | Campus
planning—Minnesota—Rochester. | Education, Higher—Aims and
objectives—United States.
Classification: LCC LD3369.5.R6 L45 2020 | DDC 378.776/155—dc23
LC record available at https://lccn.loc.gov/2020004898

A British Cataloging-in-Publication record for this book is available from the
British Library.

♾ The paper used in this publication meets the requirements of the American
National Standard for Information Sciences—Permanence of Paper for Printed
Library Materials, ANSI Z39.48-1992.

www.rutgersuniversitypress.org

Manufactured in the United States of America

This book is dedicated to the students. My frequent interactions with students at the University of Minnesota Rochester truly enriched my life. I will always be deeply indebted to them for how they modeled knowing and becoming.

Over forty years ago, I became a faculty member because I wanted to make the world a better place. I idealistically believed, and naively, that we would solve the problems of the world through our research. So I devoted the first twenty years of my career studying how the brain works—how we encode, perceive, and interact with the world. Understanding the brain and cognition is how I would contribute to making the world a better place.

Today, I understand more about the brain and cognition than I did forty years ago. And I did not solve the problems of the world. Making the world a better place is a journey without a destination. What I learned is that the real solution to addressing global challenges is to perpetuate the journey through our students.

As educators, we are given a gift to witness the power of human potential. We engage, interact, nurture, and challenge students—develop their potential. They grow from their missteps. They learn how to embrace life's complexities. They become empathetic and deeply care about others. And we begin to see in them the promising signs of continuing the journey of making the world a better place. This book is dedicated to them. The world's future is in good hands.

Contents

Preface

I served as the inaugural chancellor of the University of Minnesota Rochester (UMR), a new campus which became part of the University of Minnesota System in 2006. When I retired as its chancellor in August 2017, many of my colleagues urged me to write about my experiences starting a campus from scratch. They wanted me to write the UMR story.

But the UMR story is still being written today. UMR is just over a decade old and is very young in campus years. It has learned to crawl, and it is just beginning to learn how to walk. Many want it to run with its vision and purpose.

It would be premature to write the UMR story, nor am I the right person to write it. With the campus being very young, the UMR story is still evolving and is being written daily by the faculty, staff, students, administrators, and community stakeholders, all dedicated to developing human potential. The new chancellor, Lori Carrell, who was the vice chancellor for academic affairs and student development for about half of my tenure as the chancellor, is continuing to write the story with all her coauthors as she leads UMR through its strategic growth phase.

As I considered writing the UMR story, I realized that my experiences as a leader of a brand new campus were unique and created an extraordinary opportunity to view higher education through a different lens. When nurturing a new campus, the inaugural leader must come to grips with why it exists and what is its purpose.

This question is not faced by new leaders at established campuses. The search for a new leader at an established campus is shaped by its mission. The search process is designed to attract and select someone whose demeanor aligns with its historical mission and who possesses the managerial and operational expertise to address the administrative and fiscal challenges associated with executing the campus mission.

Not only does the campus mission shape the leadership on an established campus, it also serves to direct its future in strategic planning. A strategic planning process typically begins with the assumption that the mission is a given. The campus mission is often expressed as an immutable proclamation in a mission statement. "The University of Place will make the world better by its teaching, research, and service." Any strategic debate tends to focus on a vision, or how the campus mission should manifest itself in the future.

But vision statements, being aspirational, also tend to be very general. "The University of Place will be recognized for making its region, its state, and the nation an outstanding place by its life-changing teaching, by its innovative research to enhance health and new business formation, and by its active engagement with its community to solve societal problems."

My experience as a participant in many strategic planning exercises is that we as leaders rarely engage in substantive discussions about mission. We are apt to honor legacy and the words written by the founders. We shy away from difficult conversations about why this mission or even if we can execute the mission in the rapidly and ever-changing landscape of higher education. We are not shy to move from these difficult discussions onto tactics. Fiscal issues are real and immediate. We are quickly consumed by topics like operational efficiency, revenue generation, and budget cutting. In a perverse way over the last several decades, core aspects of campus planning have been hijacked by financial worries.

When a strategic planning group is pushed to examine a mission statement, often at the chiding by a consultant, I notice a tendency among higher education leaders to interpret mission statements freely and without prioritization to justify the full spectrum of current campus activities. These discussions tend to evolve into an artful backfill, where a strategic planning group generates a consensus around the best way (best argument, best interpretation, best choice of words) to connect all we do with the mission statement. "The reason the campus exists is to . . ." Often our strategic planning process provides a license to liberally fill in the blank.

A historical mission originally shaped a campus identity by providing a rationale for its existence. I understand why leaders continue to honor a campus heritage through its mission statement. However, we also need today more specific and contemporary answers than those provided by a mission derived at a different time to address a different set of human needs. We need a twenty-first-century version of the mission in order to more effectively address human needs today: Why does the campus exist today? What is its rationale today? This is campus purpose.

Establishing a campus purpose is imperative for a leader of a nascent campus. A new campus does not have a legacy mission, nor does the new campus have any ongoing activities to define its identity. It is completely untethered. The dangers associated with failing to establish a campus purpose are graver for a new campus. Without a campus purpose, its identity would be unstable and serendipitously shaped by activities driven by the issue du jour or shaped by the whims of others.

When I first arrived in Rochester, I heard many views about what the new campus should do and how it should do it. You need to compete and generate large enrollments, build classrooms, laboratories, a student center, dormitories, athletic fields and venues, a performing arts center, offer online learning to adults, support start-up businesses, conduct applied research, and so on. Without a shared understanding of purpose, the scope of a new campus naturally expands at an unsustainable rate as we try to be all things to all people.

I could not start with tactics, programs, or operations. When building a campus from scratch, I had to face the question, Why does the campus exist? and define a campus purpose during its embryonic stage. A clear answer to this why question was needed before I even thought about what the campus should do or how it should do it. The campus purpose must drive decisions about infrastructure, institutional design, scope, and programs. It must prioritize campus activities.

This is not to say that a focus on purpose will immunize a brand new campus to the fiscal woes of higher education. Financial resources will still set the parameters for how you do it or how much you do. What you do must align with why you do it because of who you are. I have often articulated this concept by saying that bigger is not better, but better is better. In other words, one can optimize campus purpose within an environment of constrained resources through setting program scope and campus size.

As a leader of a budding campus, I knew that I must first engage groups in conversations about campus purpose, and redirect the discussion from the "whats" and the "hows" to why the campus exists. This is the story that I share in the book.

It is not the UMR story, but rather a story launching a brand new campus with a defined purpose. It is a story about how campus purpose can inform decisions defining institutional scope; hiring faculty, staff, and administrators; launching new degree programs; managing space and new facilities; prioritizing initiatives and activities; operating efficiently; and managing fiscal resources. I discovered during my tenure as chancellor that a focus on campus purpose creates new and fresh ways to think about many elements of campus operation and function. It is also a story about my struggles to protect a campus purpose from being part of a pervasive higher education culture hardened by history and habit.

The reason for sharing my story about starting a campus from scratch is not to advocate for the emerging UMR model, but to fully articulate why we did what we did. How to build a campus with purpose. This is the real value of my story as we witness the reshaping of higher education.

The story begins with my interview for the position of chancellor, where I first wrestled with campus purpose and why there was a new campus in Rochester, Minnesota.

Campus with Purpose

1

The Interview

I was in my eleventh year serving as a vice president for academic affairs at the University of Missouri System when I accepted an offer to become the chancellor at the University of Minnesota Rochester (UMR) beginning in September 2007. Ever since I accepted the offer, I have been asked why I chose to leave my position in Missouri and become the inaugural chancellor of a brand new campus located in a shopping mall in Minnesota. My impulsive response was to say that I was not fired, nor to the best of my knowledge, was I being forced out, even though I probably outlived the life expectancy of a vice presidency.

My full answer was more complex, and probably one that I could not articulate clearly then as I can now after having the time to reflect on a decade-long journey nurturing the growth of UMR. But back in the summer of 2007 when I made the decision to move from Missouri to Minnesota, I was aware that my attraction to a new campus located in a shopping mall was intertwined with my experiences as an academic leader in a large university state system. These experiences in Missouri shaped my view about the future of higher education, my evolving conception about leadership, and my aspiration to be a change leader who would contribute to transformation in higher education.

My learning experience about higher education was both broad and deep during my vice presidency between 1995 and 2007. I worked closely with many leaders, at many different levels, at a variety of educational institutions. I served under five system presidents. With four campuses in the university system, I had the privilege to learn from campus chancellors, vice chancellors for academic affairs or provosts, chief research officers, campus librarians, student affairs leaders, recruitment officers, and faculty and student governance leaders. I also worked directly with members of a university board.

My portfolio also included working closely with other leaders in higher education across the state. I learned from state higher education executive officers, and presidents and vice presidents for academic affairs of two-year and four-year public and private institutions. I also interacted with state and federal legislators.

These experiences with leaders that spanned both horizontal and vertical administrative layers shaped my evolving views about the future of higher education. For example, they instilled in me the value of collaboration. I witnessed functional collaborations within a university system that achieved better administrative efficiencies and the development of joint campus initiatives to better address the educational, research, and outreach needs of the state. I observed ways that campuses with different missions worked together in synergistic ways to better serve students with swarming enrollment patterns. And I followed campus and community partnerships that benefited both the community and the campus.

I also learned about the fiscal challenges faced by campus leaders resulting from the changing mix of state-based and tuition-generated revenues. The shifting resource base often triggered budget cuts that forced leaders to discontinue academic programs. I witnessed how campus leaders struggled with the deterioration of the campus infrastructure because they were unable to fund maintenance and repair needs. This was a period when public trust in higher education began to decline.

As I traveled around the state of Missouri, I heard the general public begin to question the value of higher education. What is the value of liberal arts courses? Why can't my daughter or son find a good paying job after graduation? Why do universities conduct research that is unethical and contrary to my religious beliefs? Why do the universities make our lives more complex? Why should our children attend college? They leave our community to work in the big city after they graduate. These and similar questions were being asked against a backdrop of significant increases in tuition and burgeoning student debt.

As state and federal legislators were hearing these questions asked by their constituents, they began to call for more accountability in higher education. During my time in Missouri, the campuses were beginning to respond with strategies to improve graduation rates, measure learning outcomes, and lower tuition increases. These and other efforts to bolster public confidence in higher education continue today.

While working on these emerging challenges, I noted that leaders held different views about the reasons for the current turbulence in higher education and their views shaped how they approached the challenges. I found myself sorting leaders into two broad categories. The first group I referred to as custodial leaders, who wanted to maintain status quo. They focused their efforts on operating cleanly and efficiently. They believed that the current challenges were transitory. The custodial leaders tended to tactically tinker around institutional margins while waiting for more favorable and better fiscal times to return. My second category was change leaders, who believed that institutional transformation was necessary to adapt to the changing future. They focused their efforts on change management.

I also observed that the life of a change leader was more difficult. The change leaders were managing turmoil, often attributed to them, because they were leading change by discontinuing some things and starting new things. The custodial leaders, who tended to defend the current culture and prevailing habits to keep their campus communities in their comfort zones, dealt with less chaos and attributed current hardships to transitory external forces. Even though change was the harder path, I was attracted to the dynamic change leaders.

Toward the end of my tenure as a vice president, I was asked to serve as interim chancellor on one of the university campuses. I served in this transitional leadership role for about eight months. As a campus chief executive officer, I worked directly, closely, and continuously with the same cohorts of faculty, students, administrative leaders, staff, and community stakeholders. I greatly enjoyed these recurring interactions on a campus and felt that my prior system experiences prepared me well for the more intimate role of a campus leader. At the end of my term as an interim campus chancellor, I concluded that it was time for me to fly at a lower altitude and move from being a leader at a system level to a leader on a campus.

So, I availed myself to searches for campus presidents and chancellors. Like many other leaders who have participated in a search at this level, my experiences were frustrating, messy, ambiguous, disconcerting for my co-workers, and filled with a roller coaster of emotions. Although search firms reassured me that my interview experiences were typical, I ate a lot of humble pie during this phase of my career.

This was my state of mind when a search firm contacted me about a chancellor position for a brand new campus in Rochester, Minnesota. I didn't know the campus so I asked the search consultant to describe the institution. He told me University of Minnesota Board of Regents recently approved a new campus to be located in Rochester, making it the fifth campus of the university system. He also indicated that the state legislature appropriated funds to launch and support the ongoing operation of the campus. The search consultant had my attention, and I was excited about the possibility at this point in our conversation.

He then shared with me that the new campus was located in a shopping mall. My excitement level dropped immediately. His comment about the shopping mall triggered in me a concern about the level of commitment by the board and by the state to begin a new public campus. Starting a new public university, especially in the Midwest, was unheard of since student enrollments and state funding are projected to both decline over the next several decades.

I then asked if there were any students enrolled in classes at the new site. He said about 400, which was much less than the current enrollment of 60,000 students at the University of Missouri. I asked about a projected enrollment for the new campus. The search consultant responded that he believed that the future enrollment was yet to be determined, which again fueled my concerns about the seriousness of the public commitment to the new campus.

I asked about degree programs. The search consultant said that the campus did not yet have its own programs but around twenty programs were being delivered on site in Rochester by the other campuses of the University of Minnesota. I asked if they knew what kind of programs they intended to eventually offer at the new campus. The search consultant mentioned a report to the governor written by a group of local community leaders. In the report, the community listed three programmatic areas for the new campus: health sciences, biotechnology, and nanotechnology. I responded that these areas were exciting and growing fields, but each was very expensive to mount and operate.

This led me to my follow-up questions about sources and level of funding for the new campus. The consultant mentioned that one-time funds were committed by the City of Rochester for the new campus, which, to my knowledge, is a very uncommon source of funding for a higher education institution. This was impressive.

The search consultant also mentioned the important role of fund-raising by the inaugural chancellor, but all search consultants talk about the importance of fund-raising to any candidate for any presidency, as if fund-raising of nonrecurring resources is the magic bullet that will rid a campus of its financial challenges. However, at a new campus the chancellor needs to build a fund-raising organization from scratch. This is difficult because there are no alumni. And the new chancellor would be soliciting funds solely based on ideas without the trust and commitment accumulated from relationships steeped in the history of the campus.

What concerned me the most was the level of recurring funding provided by the state. It was insufficient to operate undergraduate, graduate, and research programs in the proposed programmatic areas. It also seemed to me that a shopping mall was not an ideal facility to attract and recruit faculty in competitive fields like biotechnology and nanotechnology. The immediate challenge of the inaugural chancellor would be to calibrate expectations and align aspirations with resources, which would be a tough conversation deflating the dreams of a committed community who worked tirelessly for years to get a public campus located in Rochester.

Toward the end of our phone conversation, I shared with the search consultant that there didn't seem to be much coordinated planning for the new campus that aligned programmatic aspirations with its site and funding levels. What I did not share with the consultant was my sense that the decision to launch a new campus in Minnesota was driven more by politics than by programmatic need.

I ended the phone conversation with the search consultant with a polite thanks, but a shopping mall, 400 students, and unrealistic expectations? I really had something else in mind.

The search consultant was persistent and continued to call. Maybe I was vulnerable from being in a humbling phase of my search journey. For whatever reason, I decided to submit an application. This was not difficult since I had plenty of practice and prepared materials from submitting applications for other campus leadership positions. Fortunately, I became a finalist.

The finalists' interviews were both in the Twin Cities, the location of the university system office and the large comprehensive research campus, and in Rochester. What I remember most about the interviews in the Twin Cities was the polar opposite nature of the conversations. In one set of meetings, I met with deans, department chairs, and leaders of central administrative units. They asked me repeatedly to justify why the University of Minnesota was starting a new campus. Didn't I know that I was taking precious resources away from other campuses, colleges, and schools? I had to bite my tongue during these interrogations—the meetings did not feel like an interview. "I" did not make the decision to start a new campus and was not privy to all the prior history surrounding the decision, which made it difficult for me to directly address their question.

Nonetheless, I tried to switch the conversation to the possible return on investment in the new campus to the university overall, which I could tell by their nonverbals did not resonate well with the interviewers. I fully understood why the academic and administrative leaders asked their questions with frustration. They were struggling with tough decisions related to significant budget cuts. I was making similar tough decisions in Missouri.

At the end of the morning interviews with the academic and administrative leaders, I remember thinking to myself, "I really have something else in mind." During the afternoon, I met with the current president of the University of Minnesota. He talked about innovation and partnership, the importance of making an investment in Rochester, and its return to the University of Minnesota and to the state's economy. He described the leadership opportunity in Rochester as a blank slate and was not surprised that different groups would have different expectations for the campus. The president had something else in mind.

He acknowledged that the mass and inertia of culture and habit at large, established institutions impeded transformation in higher education. He believed that a smaller, new institution would have the nimbleness to try new models, which could inform larger, established institutions about better and more efficient ways to run a campus. The president told me he was looking for an innovative leader who would fully leverage the unique opportunity to start a campus from scratch. The president was a change leader, and creating a new campus was his strategy to implement change. This conversation resonated with me at my core. Without it, I likely would not have continued the interview on the next day in Rochester.

When I arrived in Rochester, my visit began with a tour of the upper two floors of the shopping mall that were under renovation to be the future site of UMR. The first walk through did not allay my concerns about a shopping mall being the site for the new campus.

Later that morning during a break between interviews, I walked around the downtown area. It was much more substantial than I expected for a city with a population around 100,000. There was a large public library, civic center, art center, large park, river walks, a variety of stores and shops, restaurants, hotels, urban living spaces, and many other amenities that you tend to find in larger urban communities. I later heard Rochester described as a small town with large city assets. Then there was the Mayo Clinic and its expansive complex. All of this was within a short walking distance of the shopping mall.

As I continued my walk, I realized that the surprising mixture of commerce and facilities in the compact downtown area existed to support the millions of patients and visitors who travel to Rochester each year for their health care at the Mayo Clinic. I later learned that the Mayo Clinic employs more than 30,000 at its downtown Rochester site, and there was a daily influx of thousands of patients and visitors. This density of people gave the downtown area its urban feel, but at the same time the small residential population of Rochester made the area feel intimate and friendly.

In the afternoon, I gave a presentation about the challenges of higher education to the general public, which I had given before during other interviews. After the presentation, I interacted with the audience and responded to their questions. It was during this time that I met with members of the Rochester community. Their commitment to the new campus was something that I never witnessed before, even on campuses with active and connected alumni. A key group of the Rochester stakeholders, who I later referred to as the UMR Originators, espoused a deep and personal ownership of their new campus and they were completely vested in its successful launch. I learned later that it was the UMR Originators who lobbied the city council for the allocation of city funds to assist in the launch of the new campus.

On the return flight to Missouri, I contemplated the interviews, the shopping mall, my walking tour of the downtown, my interactions with the community, my conversation with the president, and the chancellor position. My first thoughts were still, "I really have something else in mind." I expected at some point to lead a moderate size campus like those I had visited many times in Missouri. But as my mind wandered during the flight, I began to reflect about my career over the past eleven years as a system vice president working with leaders at established institutions. It occurred to me that I was spending all my time managing change. If I accepted a leadership position at another established institution, I would continue managing change.

In Rochester, I would be leading a new institution. Without question, the inaugural chancellor of a new campus would have a major impact. And reflecting on my conversation with the president of the university, this place would be an incredible opportunity for a change leader. Here I could create change, not manage change.

I began to realize that Rochester was a place where I could tap into my intuition about higher education that I developed over the last decade. It was a place where I could possibly create the future university today—one that has a sustainable cost structure, shaped by a new approach to learning that prepares all students for the future, and values partnerships with the university system offices, other higher education institutions, and the community.

I began to think about the shopping mall differently. When I toured, I remember visiting the space that was designated to become the chancellor's office. The space overlooked a downtown plaza with a great view of the main building of the Mayo Clinic. The chancellor's office was located in the center of, what many refer to as, the "City for Health."

The shopping mall was a vibrant hub of the skyway system. Thousands of health care and business professionals, and the 2.8 million patients and visitors from all over the United States and the world who traveled to the Mayo Clinic each year, walked through this space on a daily basis. The new campus, because of its location, was in the center of this vibrancy.

As my mind continued to wander, I imagined how the new campus was a core part of the city and its downtown, where the campus borders would be difficult to delineate. You would see a little of the campus here, a little of it over there. A campus tour would be much more than a walk across a quad, but a tour of the dynamic hub of the international City for Health.

My thoughts continued about how the campus could partner with the downtown community for student recreation, student housing, student health services, and for community engagement and problem-based learning. The students would roam the City for Health and could interact with leaders and personnel from Mayo Clinic, IBM, bank offices, small businesses, and the arts community. I imagined creative collisions between students and the professionals they aspired to become. I daydreamed about a truly deep integration of the campus into its community, not only physically but also programmatically.

At some point during the flight back to Missouri, my thoughts about the chancellor position at UMR switched from being about a job to being about a real opportunity for a change leader. How many leaders have the opportunity to build a campus from scratch with a brand name of a major research university, like the University of Minnesota? My musings went from "I really have something else in mind" to a real opportunity for a change leader to make a positive impact on higher education.

But then my excitement about this unique leadership opportunity gave way to trepidation. The impact of a change leader at this new campus, whether positive or negative, would be immediate and long lasting, if not permanent. Given the ambiguity around the initial planning and expectations for the new campus, a strategic miscalculation could result in the closing of the budding campus. The campus was in a critical stage of development. What happened during its first years of existence would have a long-lasting impact on how it functioned over its lifetime.

I studied critical periods of development in the brain many years ago during my postdoctoral fellowship. There is a critical period in the early development of the brain when the experiences of the organism within a limited time frame have a long-lasting, in many cases permanent, impact on how the brain is organized and how it functions. In a similar way, UMR, being a brand new campus during its formative stage, was in a critical period of development.

My apprehension centered on the high risks facing a change leader of a campus that was in a critical period of development. As a vice president, I considered myself a strategic risk taker, open to explore new innovations. Over the eleven years that I served as vice president, I launched innovative programs and initiatives that failed, which is expected when being entrepreneurial. In fact, I learned during my time in Missouri that my biggest mistake was not failing, but not failing fast. The risk of failure was comparatively small. The program or initiative would simply be discontinued, with some loss of time and money.

But the risks are much higher for a new institution with shallow roots. It might not be able to survive a strategic hiccup. This scared me. My fears were further deepened when I considered the uncertainty around the prior planning for the new campus. It was not clear to me, certainly not after just a two-day visit, whether the local community, the University of Minnesota, and the state shared a common understanding about the future direction of its new campus.

My colleagues who fell in the custodial leader category would probably advise me to take the safe route and build a campus using the standard university playbook. The dilemma of a safe approach was that a standard campus was duplicative in a region where projections of future student enrollments are diminishing. I rejected the so-called safe, franchise campus approach. It was a strategic recipe for the eventual demise and closure of the campus.

It was within this context that I recalled my interview with the president. I was deeply impacted by the rationale of the president for launching the new campus. I agreed with him that the new campus in Rochester needed a change leader who shaped it so it was distinctive and added unique value to the university system, the state, and the city.

My fears about the high stakes for a change leader at a brand new campus subsided somewhat when I realized that I was obsessing about what the new campus would do and how it would do it.

Rather, a change leader must immediately focus on why the new campus exists, its rationale, and its purpose. A distinctive campus purpose will sustain the new campus in the long term.

If I was fortunate to be offered and bold enough to accept this leadership opportunity, I needed to leverage my decade-long experiences as a vice president and use my intuition about higher education and its future to establish a distinctive purpose for the new campus. Then I needed to be relentless during its formative years focusing on quality and a culture of innovation and improvement, traits that would be immutable and hardwired into the developing nervous system of the infant campus. In this way, the future administration, faculty, staff, and students could define and redefine "hows" and "whats" for its "why" (purpose) during its growth.

My job as its leader was to establish a clear and distinctive purpose for the campus and to preserve its adaptability. A distinctive purpose with an openness and a flexibility to be creative and innovative would sustain the new campus over the long term. This was the best strategic recipe to develop a new campus during its formative stage. My rushing thoughts about the leadership challenges in building a campus from scratch were interrupted as the pilot announced to prepare for the landing at the St. Louis airport.

I was back at the airport a few weeks later to travel to a meeting about undergraduate student learning when I received a call from a vice president at the University of Minnesota. Unlike my prior interviews for leadership openings, this one had a happy ending for me. I was invited to be the inaugural chancellor of UMR. The rest of the book tells my story about starting a new campus.

2

Why Does the New Campus Exist?

During the summer prior to departing for Rochester, I chatted with my leadership colleagues in Missouri about my new chancellor position. I asked them how they would resolve the ambiguity concerning the purpose of the new campus in Minnesota. I was also very interested in their thoughts about the challenges leading a new campus with shallow roots. Most said they did not have any specific advice for me, which was not surprising since very few new campuses were launched during their tenure as leaders in higher education. Some were excited about the position and believed it was a unique leadership experience. Others were cautious and concerned. They worried about sustaining a new campus in the current environment without historical political and financial bases of support.

As I listened to their thoughts about starting a campus from scratch, I again found myself categorizing their feedback into the same two broad categories which I had used to group their approaches to the current challenges at their established institutions.

My colleagues who fell in the custodial leader category tended to favor a franchise approach that would leverage the brand of the University of Minnesota. They advised me to build the campus so it looked and felt like a smaller version of the large comprehensive campus in the Twin Cities. They believed that this was the safest path forward.

But building a typical campus from scratch with a breadth of programs, student dormitories, campus quad, student activities and recreation, intercollegiate athletics, and so on, was a major investment and not affordable. A quick back-of-an-envelope estimate of the overall cost to assemble the infrastructure and to hire the faculty and staff for a moderate size institution could be hundreds of millions of dollars. Such an investment was simply out of range and not fathomed by anyone given the current funding environment for higher education. State funding for higher education is projected to continue to decrease, there will not be financially established alumni from whom to solicit support for many years, and the new campus is located in a small-to-medium size city with limited resources. More importantly, a typical campus was duplicative in a region where projections of future student enrollments are diminishing. It became quickly evident that a franchise campus approach was a strategic recipe for the rapid demise of the campus.

My colleagues who I viewed as change leaders saw the opportunity to build a campus from scratch differently. Their perspective reminded me of my conversation with the president during the interview. They believed that launching a new campus enabled a leader to create change without all the emotional and operational transaction costs associated with undoing things (institutional unlearning) and starting new things (institutional re-learning) that they experienced at their established institutions. At a brand new campus, the leader could focus on creating change without the burden of managing change. The change leaders believed that starting a campus from scratch was a unique opportunity to build something special and distinctive. They felt that a new campus with the right distinctive signature would be sustainable in the long term. My colleagues in the change leader category convinced me that my first task as the new chancellor was to discover what would make UMR distinctive and special.

When I arrived in Rochester in the fall 2007, I was immediately immersed in a welcoming and listening tour. I met with leaders from the University of Minnesota; the Mayo Clinic; the state, county, and city; and regional civic and business organizations. One of my early meetings was with a group of community leaders who were the authors of the report to the governor justifying the creation of a new campus in Rochester. There would have been no UMR without the politically astute and persistent efforts by the UMR Originators. In their report, they suggested that the new campus should have three programmatic areas: health sciences, biotechnology, and nanotechnology.

I was looking forward to meeting with the UMR Originators to better understand why they included these programmatic areas in the governor's report. These three areas of programming were never mentioned to me during any of my interviews with the leaders at the University of Minnesota. The vice president overseeing the university system operation and the president did mention that it would be important for UMR to develop partnerships with the Mayo Clinic and with IBM, both with locations in Rochester. Their proximity provided a rationale to pursue health sciences and biotechnology programs.

When I met with the UMR Originators, we chatted about their report to the governor and their recommended programmatic direction for the new campus. As we discussed campus programming, somewhat surprisingly, they did not seem wedded to any specific programs or even to a specific programmatic plan for the campus. Rather, I was struck by their practicality for launching a new campus. It seemed as though they had surpassed the political hurdle to get a new campus located in Rochester and now they were focused on practical issues associated with starting the campus.

I also discovered in other stakeholder meetings that there was not a shared understanding about the programmatic future of UMR. Some thought that the new campus would only serve adults with graduate programming. Some thought that UMR would only offer allied health programs. Some thought that UMR would be an online university and a shadow operation of the academic health center in the Twin Cities.

And there were other understandings. Today, I believe that these malleable expectations about campus programming was a by-product of the political strategy deployed to garner broad support for a new campus at the state level and at the University of Minnesota. The political dynamic shaped a chameleon narrative for the proposed new campus. The future campus would change its programmatic colors and blend in differently for different audiences so as to minimize any disturbance to the ecosystem of Minnesota higher education. The future campus would provide something for everyone, but the future campus would also not have the something that would make it duplicative or competitive.

As a result, there was no consensus about the programmatic direction for the new campus, which was a relief to me. I was worried that I had to deflate the dreams of an entire community and realign their programmatic expectations to be commensurate with the funding outlook for the new campus. For example, I knew that the new campus did not have the resources to launch a research program in nanotechnology, or build nationally ranked research/graduate programs in the health sciences.

Although there was no agreement on the programmatic future, many stakeholders did agree that the new campus must be special and top-notch. This character for the new campus was uniformly pressed by the UMR Originators. They insisted that UMR be "world class." I remember a member of the UMR Originators asking me when my strategic plan to make UMR world class would be finished. His question caught me by surprise. So I asked him and other Originators to help me better understand what they meant by world class. Although they did not present a precise definition, it was clear from the discussion that they wanted UMR to be distinctive and recognized widely and favorably for what it does. Their comments reminded me of the advice shared with me by the change leaders in Missouri.

There were some stakeholders who were disappointed that UMR did not launch, as an example, a nanotechnology program. However, overall what I consistently heard during my welcoming and listening tour was that the new campus must be special, top-notch, and world class. The stakeholders cared more about these qualities than any specific program.

After completing my welcoming and listening tour, I now felt that I could move away from a discussion about specific degree programs and focus on more general questions about the purpose of UMR. I began to ask, "Why does this campus exist?"

Some answered the question by saying that the new campus brings new business to the region. Others answered that the new campus generates new construction in the downtown area. Some said that the new campus brings new kinds of entertainment to Rochester through its intercollegiate sports programs and arts performances. Some answered that the research activity of the new campus attracts new start-up companies to the city.

I heard from local politicians that the reason that the campus exists is because Rochester deserves one. It was about time the third largest city in the state had its own public, four-year campus. I also heard from our state legislators that the new campus does not drain state resources.

I heard that the new campus exists to provide employment for many professionals who live in Rochester, many of whom were trailing spouses with graduate degrees. The campus exists to retain professional talent in a smaller city.

I also heard from faculty and academic administrators at other institutions that the campus exists to collaborate with their institution and provide a new venue to offer their programs and courses to local residents, either through face-to-face, online, or hybrid instruction. But I also heard from this group that the campus does not exist to offer duplicative programs that would encroach on their enrollments.

Many others gave their views about why the campus exists. As I struggled to decipher their answers, I realized that the campus stakeholders were sharing their views about what the campus should do or how it should do it, but less, if at all, about why the campus exists. Maybe I did not ask the question in the right way or direct the conversation to better garner their views about campus purpose. On further reflection about the stakeholder comments, I was not really surprised by the assorted nature of their responses.

Leaders at established higher education institutions tend to let what they do and how they do it define who they are. They also struggle with questions about purpose and why a campus exists. We, as leaders in higher education, have become opportunistic, especially during these lean fiscal times. As a consequence, we market our campuses to be all things to all people.

This expansive view about the purpose of a campus has become the norm, and the public instinctively expects much from higher education. This might be why the chameleon political strategy to garner support for a new campus was successful and why there are broad expectations about the future of the new campus in Rochester. An expansive view about the purpose of UMR is just a symptom of a general persona projected today by higher education.

Initially, I was frustrated with my effort to determine why the campus exists. I did not think that the wide-ranging stakeholders' views were very helpful in determining a campus purpose. I knew that I had to establish a more specific campus purpose. Otherwise, the emerging campus activities would be serendipitous, disjointed, and not special and world class, as demanded by the UMR Originators. It would be a very unhealthy state for a campus during its critical period of development. I needed somehow to establish a campus purpose.

I decided to re-examine the stakeholders' comments using a thematic approach to search for any attributes of a campus purpose that might be embedded in their comments. Then I planned to use these attributes to define a campus purpose.

I first put aside the political reasons why the new campus exists. These political-based views are not informative about campus purpose, since the primary rationale for establishing a new publicly supported campus in Rochester was that the city deserved one.

But in reviewing the other expectations for the new campus, I discovered three categories of attributes for the campus purpose: campus calling, campus distinctiveness, and campus rationale.

I heard most clearly from the UMR Originators that the campus calling was to be world class. Whatever UMR does must be recognized widely and favorably. UMR was next door to an internationally recognized health care institution and shared a city with a significant IBM facility with a global reputation. It was the expectation of the Rochester community that its newest major institution, UMR, was also world class and recognized widely for its special contributions.

I heard most clearly from my colleagues who were change leaders in Missouri and from the president of the university that the new campus must be distinctive. The new campus must have a focused and unique programmatic signature. Its uniqueness will sustain and nurture the campus in the long term.

And I heard most clearly from leaders at the University of Minnesota and other Minnesota higher education institutions that the only rationale for a new campus was to add value. The new campus must not duplicate services or programs, but add unique value to the community, the state, and to the University of Minnesota.

I also realized that these three attributes about campus purpose were interrelated operationally. The resources did not exist to be all things to all people. If UMR was to be distinctive and world class, I needed to develop a special niche and direct investments to support the niche.

At this stage of my thinking about why the campus exists, I believed that determining a distinctive niche that added value to the Rochester community and to the University of Minnesota would begin to define a campus purpose. How can the campus add value to the Rochester community? How can the campus add value to the University of Minnesota?

What did the Rochester community need? There was already a higher education presence in the community with more than 10,000 post-secondary students participating in the current eco-system of higher education in a city with a population a little over 100,000. But a majority of these students were residents of Rochester, and many were adults attending college part time. What Rochester needed was a campus that would attract to the area younger talent (eighteen- to twenty-two-year-olds) to relocate, live in, and become immersed in a region with a voracious appetite for a health-based workforce.

The health-based workforce needs already outstripped the population of Rochester. There were busloads of Mayo employees traveling back and forth from their homes in different regions of Minnesota, Iowa, and Wisconsin to Rochester on a daily basis in order to meet the workforce needs in health care. The future demand for health care workers across the nation is projected to grow for decades. Given the historical and projected growth for the Mayo Clinic, meeting the extraordinary demand for health care workers was a critical success factor for Rochester's future economy.

In addition to attracting talent from outside the region to Rochester, UMR could leverage the existing network of talent in the community to enrich the learning opportunities for students interested in health care. The Mayo Clinic and downtown Rochester composes what is internationally recognized as the "City for Health." UMR could achieve world class by working with world class organizations.

But just offering health science programs was not distinctive. Many established institutions offered health science degrees at the undergraduate, graduate, and professional levels. What would make UMR distinctive is to be an undergraduate health science campus that was specially designed for undergraduate students who have a passion to care for others and who need to discover the best way for them to manifest their passion. At an undergraduate health science campus, all the students would share a common passion to care for others in a variety of patient- and non-patient-based health care settings. A shared career trajectory would bond students together.

UMR could focus on only *one* undergraduate program in the health sciences that would serve as a springboard for students to pursue a variety of health-related careers. A single degree program in the health sciences contrasted with the many degree programs offered by an established institution, where its pre-health undergraduate programs were a small part of their overall degree program portfolio. UMR's singular programmatic focus would make it special and distinctive.

The curriculum at an undergraduate health science campus could be specially designed to leverage a common interest in the health sciences, with all the courses having a health science connection. The math, chemistry, sociology, history, philosophy, physics, writing, language, and humanities courses would be connected by using related health topics. There would not be any health science courses per se, because health was embedded in all the courses and taught through the lens of an academic discipline.

For example, the math faculty could teach statistics by asking students to use national public health data resources to answer questions like, How much does one need to increase the price for a pack of cigarettes to reduce the cancer rate by 50 percent in the US? Or the sociology faculty could engage students in a study of addiction by connecting their answers to the statistics question and examine why increasing the cost of cigarettes has a marginal effect on smoking rates. Or the chemistry teacher could connect by teaching the chemistry of smoking, the molecular composition of nicotine, and why nicotine replacements can emulate the effects of smoking. Or the writing faculty could connect by working with the students when they are writing their joint papers for sociology and math courses about smoking, addiction, and cancer rates. Or the philosophy faculty could connect by engaging the students in issues of ethics underlying antismoking efforts. Or the physics teacher could connect by describing the physics underlying radiation treatment for cancer or X-ray diagnosis of lung cancer. Or a language teacher could connect by designing the grammatical and vocabulary exercises in Spanish so students can engage in a conversation with someone in Spanish about medical diagnosis and treatment of cancer.

One UMR student used this metaphor to explain her understanding of the integrated curriculum connected by health topics. She said that UMR students learned that a health issue is not a biology problem. It is not a mathematics problem. It is not a philosophy problem. Nor a sociology problem. It is a health problem. She believed that the best way to understand a health issue was to view it from different perspectives by comparing, contrasting, and combining how a biologist approached a health issue, how a philosopher approached the issue, how a mathematician approached it, how a sociologist approached the issue, and so on. She said that a connected curriculum was like a stir-fry. A stir-fry recipe combines foods with different flavors and textures. The combination enriches the flavors of the individual ingredients by accentuating the flavor and texture contrasts. A seasoning links all the ingredients. She said the integrated curriculum in a similar way enriched the learning about health by connecting different disciplinary flavors with the seasoning of a health topic.

This would be a special and distinctive curricular experience for undergraduate students. At established institutions, undergraduates who were interested in the health sciences took general education courses without a cross-course, cross-disciplinary health connection. It was only in major courses where intentional discussions about health sciences typically occurred.

Moreover, given the special location of UMR in the City for Health, undergraduate students at UMR, first-year students through seniors, could avail themselves to distinctive clinical experiences as volunteers, as work-study students, and through connected course work at the Mayo Clinic. "Leverage Our Place" is one of the principles articulated by Michael Crow and William Dabars in their book *Designing the New American University*.[1]

The students could volunteer at the Ronald McDonald House and interact with parents and with their children who are undergoing medical treatments. They could volunteer at the local hospice facility interacting with patients and families during a very special time in their lives. They could volunteer by giving hand massages to relax patients awaiting a chemo treatment. They could volunteer in an office that designs and constructs prosthetics tailored to address the unique needs of a patient. They could volunteer to play guitar and sing for patients in the hospital in an art-by-the-bedside program. They could volunteer to work in laboratories discovering new ways to empower the patient's own immune system to kill cancer cells. They could volunteer in a laboratory modeling ways to dissolve kidney stones without surgery or sonic blasts. They could volunteer to assist medical professionals who travel to underdeveloped regions of the world and provide basic health care. They could volunteer as medical scribes and assist doctors and nurses in gathering patient information. They could volunteer to translate medical pamphlets into Spanish. They could volunteer in research projects designed to improve the patient experience during clinical visits. (These are actual examples of UMR students engaging with the City for Health).

The other special advantage for students being located in the City for Health is that they could find health-related part-time jobs. The students could obtain a Certified Nursing Assistant certificate and work in assisted living facilities, clinics, and hospitals. The students could pursue a phlebotomy certification and work drawing blood samples. Students could use their work-study grant provided to them as financial aid to partially cover their salary when working at a nonprofit entity. This would be a win-win situation for both the student and the nonprofit and open many doors for students to get clinical experience. These are examples of the special and distinctive out-of-the-classroom experiences that would be ubiquitous for undergraduate students in Rochester

A campus with an exclusive focus on undergraduate health education immersed in a mecca of health care would clearly be distinctive and world class. By being a distinctive undergraduate health campus, it could attract young talent by leveraging the amenities of the City for Health with an unquenchable thirst for a health care workforce. No other campus located in Rochester was positioned to attract from outside the area, house and immerse full-time students into the city, and support their engagement with all the clinical amenities of the City for Health as they pursued baccalaureate degrees in the health sciences. The new campus by its design would add value by addressing the health care workforce needs of the city of Rochester. This special niche in undergraduate health science education could be adequately funded by a targeted investment of the ongoing state support and projected tuition revenues.

The new campus was not only part of the city of Rochester, but it was also part of the University of Minnesota. The University of

Minnesota was making an ongoing and significant investment in its new campus in Rochester, which I heard very clearly from the deans and other senior administrators during my interviews for the position of chancellor. What was the benefit to the University of Minnesota that justified their investment in the new Rochester campus?

What did the University of Minnesota need? The University of Minnesota has one of the largest comprehensive campuses in the nation. The comprehensive nature of its Twin Cities campus was a strategic advantage. It is not easy to find a programmatic gap that needs to be filled by its new campus in Rochester.

As I deliberated how UMR could add value to the University of Minnesota, I recalled one of my last assignments in Missouri working with academic leaders from other large comprehensive campuses. When I served as senior vice president at the University of Missouri, I represented the university on a nationwide committee called Voluntary System of Accountability (VSA). The charge of the VSA committee was to develop a set of measurable learning outcomes for undergraduates that all institutions could use on a voluntary basis to assess the impact of their undergraduate instruction. The committee was formed in response to national calls for accountability in higher education. At the time, there were political discussions at the federal level about administering mandatory national tests to all college seniors, similar in purpose to those tests which were designed for elementary and secondary schools in the No Child Left Behind program.

I was very impressed by the credentials of the members of the VSA committee. Our committee also had access to a number of experts on undergraduate student learning. However, what struck me during our deliberations was how little we knew and agreed on about student learning and its measurement.

In other fields of research, there was agreement among experts about measurement. Researchers established and deployed reliable and valid measurements that enabled their research community to do their research, share their findings, and expand new knowledge.

However, when members of the VSA committee discussed student learning, I was struck by the lack of consensus about learning measurement and underwhelmed by our shared understanding about what undergraduates should learn. Clearly, we in the undergraduate learning industry have not had substantive and shared discussions about what our students should know and what our students should be able to do when they complete their undergraduate instruction. Nor have we built the measurement system to determine if our graduates know it and can do it.

My experience serving on the VSA committee, now looking back, greatly influenced my decision about how to add value to the University of Minnesota. The UMR campus would be committed to do research on student learning. This commitment would be at an institutional level—not just at a program level, not just at a department level, and not just at an individual researcher level. This commitment by the entire campus meant that all the faculty and staff would be devoted to understanding student learning. The biology faculty member would research how to structure group activities so students improve their grasp of biological processes. The philosophy faculty member would study ways for students to enhance their capacity to tolerate ambiguity. The chemistry faculty member would research how to arrange the sequence of chemistry courses so students would have a deeper understanding of chemical constructs. The mathematics faculty would research how students experience the basics of probability to better understand how to improve their grasp of statistics. The writing faculty would research how immersing writing experiences in all courses across all four years of the curriculum improves students' communication skills. And most importantly, the faculty would collectively research what students in the health sciences should know, how to measure what they know, and how their individual courses are integrated across the curriculum to achieve the overall student learning outcomes. The faculty at the new campus would not only conduct research on student learning and development, but also have the calling to share their findings about learning with colleagues at the University of Minnesota and with higher education overall. An institutional focus on student learning would be distinctive, world class, and add value to the University of Minnesota.

My conversations with my colleagues and stakeholders about why the new Rochester campus exists generated a constellation of perspectives and views about campus purpose. I was able to distill their feedback and extract three categories of attributes for a campus purpose: campus calling, campus distinctiveness, and campus rationale. The calling for the new campus was to be world class. Its distinctiveness contributed to the campus being world class, but its distinctiveness must align with its rationale for existence, which was to add value to the city of Rochester and the University of Minnesota. After doing an environmental scan about what added value to Rochester and to the University of Minnesota, and merging the qualities with being world class and distinctive, I concluded that the campus purpose for UMR was the juxtaposition of two campus commitments. First, UMR committed to offer a world-class and distinctive health sciences program to undergraduates who have a passion to care for others in patient and nonpatient settings. Second, UMR collectively committed as an institution to conduct research on student learning and development.

This campus purpose emerged prior to my inauguration as chancellor. It was my answer to the question why the campus exists—undergraduate health sciences and student learning and development. It was the theme of my inaugural address. I also stated in my address that the attributes that defined the campus purpose will also direct what we do and how we will do it: add value, be distinctive, and be world class.

At the time of my inauguration, I imagined that I had the map in the form of a campus purpose to guide me on the rest of my journey in starting a campus from scratch. The purpose would direct decisions about building the administrative structure and operation for the new campus. Although my purpose map had a clear destination marked, I discovered that many of the roads to get there were uncharted. Building a campus with distinctive and world-class commitments to student learning and development and to undergraduate health sciences was not straightforward and uniformly embraced. The next chapter of my story of starting a campus from scratch is about remaining true to a campus purpose despite struggling with the culture and prevailing habits of higher education and living in a period when the rate of change is accelerating.

3
Building a Campus with Purpose
Managing the Past and the Future

Cathy Davidson in her recent book titled *The New Education: How to Revolutionize the University to Prepare Students for a World in Flux* writes, "Every academic I know has the fantasy of going off and starting their own college or university."[1] This was the sentiment shared with me by those in my change leader category. What excited me the most about starting a new campus was the opportunity to create change rather than manage change, and not have to undo anything. I was wrong. Soon after I arrived in Rochester I discovered that I would still manage change. In order to create and sustain a campus with purpose, I would manage change in relation to the past history of higher education and anticipate change in an uncertain future.

My first realization that I would still manage change occurred during my welcoming and listening tour. I was asked to meet with a group of consultants. They were hired by the system office at the University of Minnesota to lay the groundwork for establishing a new campus. Unbeknown to me, this consulting firm started its work before I was hired as chancellor. When we met we quickly butted heads. They did not start with a campus purpose.

I remember the meetings—it was four against one (I was the one). They used the generic playbook for higher education about what campuses do and how they do it. Their playbook was written for campuses with a nondistinct purpose. My conversations with the consultants were reminiscent of the advice offered by my leadership colleagues who I referred to as custodial leaders. Both were advocating for a franchise campus in Rochester. As I argued in the previous chapter, I felt strongly that a franchise approach was a fatal mistake.

At the end of several intense discussions, one consultant said, "Let me get this straight, you want to build a university entirely focused on undergraduate student learning and development in the health sciences?" I said yes. He shook his head in disbelief and said that was not how other universities operated. After this meeting, I contacted the office at the University of Minnesota that hired the consultant group. I requested and they agreed that I should have more control over the consulting contract. I didn't recognize at the time that my experience with the consultants would foretell my challenges creating a campus with purpose.

Also during my welcoming and listening tour, I spent time with university staff located in Rochester who had worked tirelessly over the years to deliver off-site programs in Rochester offered by departments located on the campuses in the Twin Cities and in Duluth. They also offered continuing education programs by sub-contracting with faculty and experts from other institutions. The staff wanted their Rochester institution to look, operate, and have the autonomy of a full-fledged campus like other higher education institutions in the state. I had something else in mind—creating a campus with purpose.

I met with members of the existing staff during my first months on the job. I was able to open the minds of many staff to new possibilities for a campus with purpose. Nonetheless, some staff were frustrated with my approach and with my view of the campus purpose. They held their own views about the future of UMR. For some, I could not convert their thinking from the purpose being *my* purpose to being *our* purpose. So they (or we) decided to sever their relationship with UMR. I know that even ten years later, some former staff remain disappointed that I did not build a "real" university.

Cathy Davidson in her new book also traces the origins of many of our prevailing habits in higher education to the early 1900s, when the structure for higher education was designed to develop the human talent for a very different time and place in our history.[2] Throughout my career, I encountered many of these prevailing habits manifested in administrative processes and policies, in organizational structures, and in common practices. I inherited these historical mind-sets in my role as a leader dictating how I and others went about conducting our business in higher education. During my early years as an administrator, I believed that my primary role was to reference the correct policy or process that would shape a decision. During my latter years as an administrator, I felt more empowered to challenge existing policy and processes.

To illustrate my frustration with how we overly attend to policy and process, I recall a meeting involving a group of senior leaders and registrars. At this meeting, the campus chancellors and the president of the university system were considering a proposal that would enable students to pursue new minors created by combining unique courses offered by the different campuses in the system. The chancellors believed that this intercampus cooperation was a great way to leverage the university system for the benefit of the students. However, the registrars informed our group that their policies would not permit using courses offered by different campuses for a minor. What upset me was the immediate and reflexive response by my fellow chancellors and the president. They acquiesced and agreed with the registrars that we could not do it. I found the registrars' response perplexing and not substantiated. So I shouted, "Who works for whom here? We can rewrite these policies." But my protest was to no avail. The registrars held the policy trump card.

Our prevailing habits and mind-sets in higher education trigger instinctual behaviors that are not always in the best interest of students or learning. There is a sacred axiom in our business—academics, especially teaching and learning, are the sole province of the faculty. Albeit there are many upsides to the mind-set, there are some significant downsides. Let me provide two examples. The first example deals with the mind-set of governing boards.

Because teaching and learning are faculty business and not board business, board members spend most of their time engaged in discussions about nonacademic matters: building design and construction, salary increases, human resource policies, fund-raising, debt management, public relations, intercollegiate sports, and so on. The nonacademic part of the university evolves over time in the minds of board members as central, high-priority issues for the campus. As a consequence, individual board members have little exposure to, and many have only a superficial understanding of, matters pertaining to student learning and development. We should not be surprised when executing its fiduciary function, a governing board decides to invest, for example, tens of millions of dollars in a new athletic facility, but hesitates to invest much smaller amounts in additional academic advisors and mental health counselors.

I know what many are thinking—be careful what you are asking. I know that board engagement on student learning and development will be messy—student learning is a messy topic. But we know as educators that engagement is the best way for people to learn and understand. If we do not engage boards in debates on student learning, they will never fully understand the critical importance nor the rationale for investing in better ways to empower students to learn and develop. Unfortunately, our current mind-set frowns upon, if not precludes such an engagement with nonfaculty about how to prepare students for their lives and careers.

A similar dynamic exists when working with the state legislature. Given their lack of engagement and understanding about student learning and development, again our fault and not theirs, it should not surprise us that many legislators want students to receive college credit for high school work, want the degree path shortened to three years, believe that students can learn online all they need in life, and demand that we provide students workforce skills. I suspect that we have not sufficiently engaged the legislature on topics about student learning to fully understand what they mean by workforce skills.

As with the examples of intercampus minors or in our interactions with governing boards and the legislature, it is my impression that our prevailing habits trigger subliminal, knee jerk responses that dominate how we do things in higher education. We pay more homage to our legacy, and all its trimmings, than to campus purpose.

I struggled with the legacy structure of higher education in building a distinctive, world class undergraduate health campus focused on student learning and development. When I use the term "structure," I am referring collectively to legacy administrative systems, processes, policies, organizational structures, common practices, prevailing habits, inherited mind-sets, and culture and traditions—what I refer to as the "ghost of the university past."

Managing change, even for a nascent campus, is a battle with the ghost of university past. I did not want to instinctively deploy existing organizational structures or common practices but be open to examine the best ways to execute the campus purpose. The best approach may or may not be a prevailing habit, common practice, or an existing organizational structure of higher education. My fear was that if I wasn't diligent, the ghost of university past would push the campus toward being a franchise and divert it from its purpose.

I must acknowledge that I am suspicious about the ghost of the university past. I even associate the current structure in higher education with a ghost. However, it is not my intent to admonish any colleague who, being part of an established institution, operates within the current structure of higher education. There is the saying "be hard on structure, but soft on people." My colleagues care deeply about developing human potential. But not all of our existing structure cares, at least not about developing the human talent that we need today in the health sciences.

Over the ten years at UMR, I had to manage change by battling the ghost of university past. In some cases, I directly confronted the ghost by executing a new approach. Other times, I purposely hid from the ghost amid the daily chaos of running a campus. Laying low gave me time to execute a new approach for managing change. I call it "don't poke the ghost until armed." I found that I was better armed for battle with the ghost of university past if I had met individually with academic and civic leaders, and with faculty and staff, to make the case for the campus purpose. It proved to be an effective strategy to battle the ghost and protect the purpose. But it is a recurring battle because of the constant turnover of academic and civic leaders, and faculty and staff. Each always brings the ghost of university past.

I knew that I would battle the ghost to tailor the administrative and academic models and processes to achieve the campus purpose. I had to manage change resulting from the transition between a past and today. However, there is another category of change that must be simultaneously managed, and in many ways, this category of change management is more challenging. I also had to manage change for the transition between today and the future. How does a leader preserve campus purpose in the future when there is less certainty and the change is recurrent?

Many emerging trends will directly impact higher education in the near future. Other forces will emerge that will be ever-changing and nonpredictable. As the chancellor of a new campus with purpose, I must not only build a structure so the campus is true to its purpose—distinctive, world class, and value added—but I must also build a structure that is agile and adaptable to the future of higher education. In building a structure for a campus with purpose, I must not only re-examine the past but also anticipate the future.

There were several emerging trends in higher education that I observed during my time in Missouri.

Public Disinvestment in Higher Education. Students and families are now carrying more of the financial burden. For many, much of higher education is already out of their fiscal reach. I state this as a fact and not to place blame. The leaders of higher education are adjusting to less public support, which has pushed the overall enterprise to operate more efficiently and to search for alternate revenue sources. Unfortunately, and probably unavoidably, the leaders significantly increased tuition to compensate for having less public investment. A new steady state will emerge for the balance between state and federal support and tuition levels. However, it is unrealistic to expect that there will be significant new public investment in higher education in the near term, and probably, in the long term.

Creation and Dissemination of New Knowledge. The creation and dissemination of new knowledge is much more fluid than in the past, happening outside of academic department silos across disciplines, across institutions, and across sectors. Many administrative structures and processes in higher education are not aligned with the emergence of new modes of learning and research. These structures and processes are shaped by a culture of hierarchical knowledge, in which faculty experts in a certain academic department control the creation and dissemination of a subset of knowledge within an institution. The culture shapes the academic structure, such as departments and colleges, the governance systems, as well as the budgeting processes. All serve to reinforce a system based on a knowledge hierarchy.

New approaches to scholarship and research are being set into motion by the ubiquitous access to new information, the high degree of interconnectivity among individuals, and by the new role non-experts with different types of knowledge are playing in the creation and the distribution of budding knowledge. Open source educational and research networks make knowledge much more fluid and flatten the hierarchy. It is now less likely that new knowledge will be created and disseminated by one person, in a single department, at a particular time or place.

Maybe this social dynamic for knowledge creation isn't a recent phenomenon. Steven Johnson, in his book titled *Where Good Ideas Come From: The Natural History of Innovation*, writes about his historical analysis of the conditions that promote innovation.[3] He classified inventions based on how many participated and on the capitalization of the invention. He distinguished between inventions that involved a single inventor, or small coordinated teams within an organization, from those inventions that evolved through collective, distributed processes with a large number of groups working on the same problem. He also separated inventions based on innovators who intended to capitalize from the licensing and sale of the invention in the marketplace, where information flow was restrictive for proprietary reasons, from those innovators who exchange ideas freely and openly in a nonmarket space.

He found that many more inventions from 1400 to recent times originated in the quadrant that combined a distributed network of innovators working freely in a nonmarket environment—like the space created by a research university. A deeper analysis revealed that fluid communities formed to solve a particular problem; the density of the team; loose organizational structures that gravitate to the borders of different ways of thinking or academic disciplines, unlike the rigidity and hierarchical nature of academic departments; and the diversity of the backgrounds of the members of the team, all promoted more innovation and creativity.

Exponential Growth of New Knowledge. New knowledge is growing exponentially, making the useful life span of new discoveries shorter and shorter. We are living during a period in which the rate of change is accelerating, when some predict that new knowledge is expected to double every 12 hours in 2020, when 65 percent of today's grade schoolers will have jobs that do not yet exist, and when our graduates will change jobs 6–10 times before the age of 38. Some refer to this era of accelerating change as exponential times.[4] This rapid rate of change is creating an uncertain future for our graduates. It is changing the definition of learning, shifting the focus from content to developing the students' capacity to adapt and continue to learn.

This uncertainty about the future of our graduates was the topic of a book by Joseph Aoun, President of Northeastern University, titled *Robot-Proof Higher Education in the Age of Artificial Intelligence*.[5] He cites the work of economists who study the impacts of the confluence of big data, cognitive computing, and robotics. They predict that new technologies will be a threat to both low- and high-skilled jobs, any job based on prediction and algorithms. Nearly half of current jobs are said to be at risk to the automation from artificial intelligence (AI) and cognitive computing. They estimate that corporations will reduce salaries by $2 trillion annually through automation.

You may say that this is not the first time technology has transformed the workforce. We survived the industrial revolution. The difference today is the exponential rate of change, much too quickly for anyone to stay in the same job for an extended period of time.

This is the educator's dilemma. We are being asked to prepare students for jobs that don't yet exist, to solve problems we don't yet know about, using technologies not yet invented.[6]

Students Are Changing. Technological and demographic forces are changing students. They bring with them distinct life experiences reinforced by their own echo chambers that shape the way they perceive, encode, and interact with the world. This cognitive heterogeneity of our incoming students conflicts with our prevailing habit to treat all students the same.

Our current educational practices are premised on the assumption that students are much more homogeneous than they are today. Our practices are akin to assembly line approaches in which an institution over a four-year period deploys a single instructional practice in a repeatable fashion to a multitude of students. These cookie cutter practices work well when the raw materials, or what was "in their heads" as a new student, resulted from similar life experiences, common academic backgrounds, and growing up in the same culture.

Today, the raw materials are assorted, and the product cannot be constructed on an assembly line. Today's students are diverse in their cultures, in life experiences, and in academic backgrounds, and what new students bring with them in terms of knowledge and understanding is so varied it cannot be shaped and developed in a uniform fashion. Student learning must be individualized, not commoditized.

These emerging trends and the advent of new ones are rapidly reshaping higher education.

We are living in a period when the rate of change is accelerating, and continually adapting to these rapid changes will be critical to the survival for all of higher education. But living in these exponential times and adapting to these rapid changes creates a dilemma for a leader who is committed to preserve a campus purpose. How can a leader protect the new campus and its purpose from disruptive innovation?

There are many examples of disruptive innovation, in which an industry that overly focuses on its current product line and services to its customers is suddenly replaced by less expensive and more functional products or services made possible by new technologies and innovation.[7] Some argue that this type of disruptive innovation is already underway in higher education in the forms of online learning, Massive Open Online Courses (MOOCs), alternative credentialing, coding boot camps, and many other entrepreneurial ventures in higher education.[8]

Whether any of the new models will be disruptive to the core industry of higher education is an ongoing debate. We do know that higher education will be constantly responding to new pressures to change and adapt. We are living in exponential times, which means that managing change is a recurring process. This is why I struggle with the expression "institutional transformation." Using the expression implies time-limited transformation—the transformation is completed once the change has been made. If one ever thinks they have figured it out, they are doomed. Managing change is a recurrent process. To me, this is the lesson in the stories about disruptive innovation.

To manage change on a recurring basis for a campus with purpose, the leader must balance the tension between being agile and adaptive with being committed to a purpose. I attempted to balance this tension by developing a set of planning assumptions that anticipate the impacts of those trends that are emerging and be positioned to respond to the external forces that have not yet coalesced. I would use the planning assumptions to embed an adaptive property into the design of a new structure for a campus with purpose.

The adaptive planning assumptions used in the design of the structure for a campus with purpose are best captured in three quotes.

> What is known today is less important than the capacity to continue to learn more - becoming in contrast with knowing.
> —George Siemens[9]

The first quote states that learning today is about knowing and becoming—becoming a critical thinker, becoming a good communicator, becoming a team player, becoming inter culturally competent, becoming tolerant of ambiguity, becoming etc. We all could add to the list of foundational skills that will be critical for graduates to succeed during exponential times. President Aoun in his book writes: "A robot-proof model of higher education is *not* concerned solely with topping up students' minds with high-octane facts. Rather, it refits their mental engines, calibrating them with a creative mindset and the mental elasticity to invent, discover, or otherwise produce something society deems valuable."[10]

The definition of learning is changing. The way in which we prepare our students for their future, not ours, must also change. Our graduates will need a whole new set of skills. Cathy Davidson in her book states:

> All these educators dedicated to higher education reform understand how deeply we must go into our reconsideration not just of STEM education but also of the purpose and mission of college as a whole if we are going to train students to address the scale and scope of change in the world they face. The new education isn't simply a change in curriculum or the implementation

of a new kind of pedagogy. It is not just a course or a program. It is all of the above, undergirded by a new epistemology, a theory of knowledge that is deep, synthetic, active, and meaningful, with real impact in the world. In the end, the new education is also a verb, one that empowers our students with better ways to live and thrive in a complicated world.[11]

Learning today is about knowing and becoming. Higher education as an industry has so much to learn from the research on student learning and development. I cannot think of a better rationale for the existence of a campus that is committed as an institution to research on what students should know and be able to do, and how we know they can do it.

> It is not the strongest of the species that survives, nor is it the most intelligent that survives, it is the one most adaptable to change.
> —Charles Darwin[12]

The second quote is often attributed to Darwin. I could rewrite this quote using a higher education narrative. It would read: It is not the institution with the largest or most expensive student recreation center; it is not the institution that has accumulated the greatest number of star faculty or high ability students; it is not the institution that has the best sports program; but it is the institution that has developed a capacity to adapt that will survive.

Survival is compromised when limited energies are invested in activities or in areas that do not contribute to survival. If an animal does not manage its energy to optimize its food yield by hunting for or finding the right food in the right place during the right time of day, there will a limited return on the investment of its energy for its survival. In similar ways, leaders must manage energy for institutional survival.

There are two forms of institutional energy that must be managed by a leader: mental energy and physical resources. The management of physical resources is typically the centerpiece of campus planning and dominates governing board discussions. Mental energy, on the other hand, is rarely discussed. Institutional mental energy refers to what worries the campus community, what attracts their attention, how they prioritize their work, what keeps them up at night. There is a conservation of limited mental energy as there is a conservation of limited physical resources. The institution's mental energy must be properly invested for its survival. It can be misdirected and mismanaged by asking the campus community to do the wrong stuff or diluted by investing too much on stuff with low yield.

I recall a conversation with a chancellor in Missouri who had launched a very exciting strategic plan for her campus during her first year in office. During the early years of her tenure, she reaped much enthusiasm among the campus and external communities for the plan. Many members of both communities were deeply committed and worked tirelessly to implement it. The overall energy and buzz around the plan was amazing. During her fifth year, the chancellor lost the support of her campus community and she resigned her position.

I had a chance to chat with the ex-chancellor after her resignation and asked her why the energy around the strategic plan evaporated. She shared with me that at the beginning she felt that she was driving a tractor and pulling wagons full of supportive campus and community members on a very exciting journey. During the last two years, when she turned around, there were very few left in the wagons. She said that she drove the tractor too fast, and riders in the wagons fell off. They all tried to do too much too quickly. She did not manage their mental energy and conserve their enthusiasm to sustain the plan's execution.

The management of mental energy and physical resources as an adaptive strategy requires the leader to prioritize and focus on the scope of work. A leader must manage the expenditure of mental energy and ensure it is invested in high-priority, high-yield activities critical to achieving a campus purpose. This also means that a leader must consider different ways to do important but ancillary work that consumes less institutional energy, both physical and mental.

But the ghost of university past has inculcated in us a sense of autonomy—a do it on our own mentality. The tendency of many leaders at established institutions is to operate their own student financial aid; store their own books; hire their own legal counsel; and operate their own human resources, capital planning, information technology, and investment shops. These offices, sometimes referred to as back-office or centralized operations, provide important but ancillary support for the operation of a campus. Their functioning is necessary but not sufficient for the achievement of a campus purpose.

The distinct advantage of belonging to a university system is that these ancillary support functions can be outsourced to a centralized office. This allows an individual campus to invest its mental energy on those activities critical to sustaining a campus purpose during exponential times. In many cases, the outsourcing frees up physical resources to be invested in the campus purpose since the scale of operation enables a centralized office to more efficiently deliver the ancillary services. Having come from a system office, I was very open to the utilization of centralized services and always looked for ways to outsource ancillary support. This was an adaptive way to better manage not only physical resources but also mental energy.

The ghost of university past also embraces a bigger-is-better mind-set. I have described the expansive expectations about a campus regarding its programmatic activities. My examples thus far have been academic in nature. There are also expansive expectations for nonacademic areas. One is the intercollegiate athletics (see chapter 8 for a more thorough discussion about the purpose of intercollegiate athletics).

It was clear to me soon after I arrived in Rochester that many of the stakeholders expected intercollegiate sports programs. There is debate in the higher education industry about the role of intercollegiate sports.[13] Much of the debate is about the cost associated with being in the sports entertainment business. The cost debate has primarily focused on large comprehensive institutions of higher education in top tier sports markets. However, there is little debate about the financial impact of intercollegiate programs on small and medium-sized institutions. These intercollegiate sports programs are highly subsidized and divert resources from the academic mission, or in my case, from campus purpose.

I remember a conversation with a chancellor at a smaller campus who was bemoaning his challenges to fund Title IX requirements, football field repair, and coaches' salaries. I asked why he didn't discontinue the intercollegiate athletic program. He answered that it would be difficult, if not impossible, for two reasons. First, he did not want to battle the ghost of the university past on athletics. He felt his campus persona was intertwined with the intercollegiate sports program, and discontinuing sports at the campus would diminish the reputation of the campus. And second, the chancellor believed that the discontinuance of intercollegiate sports would diminish enrollments. Not that prospective students demanded to view intercollegiate athletic programs as fans, student attendance at athletic events was low, but that many prospective students wanted to participate in intercollegiate athletics. His marginal enrollments depended on student athletes. I asked my colleague if he wore my shoes would he start an intercollegiate sports program. He said absolutely not.

The battle with the ghost on athletics was easier for me starting a campus from scratch than for my colleague at a small established institution. UMR was recruiting a student who was interested in serving others in a health care setting, not participating in intercollegiate sports. The entertainment of the community through athletics is not aligned with campus purpose. Operating an intercollegiate sports programs misdirects physical resources, and managing the issues and the business aspects surrounding intercollegiate sports misdirects mental energy.

Despite this mismatch between the campus purpose and sports programs, there was still a strong cultural pull to launch an intercollegiate sports program at UMR. This penchant toward intercollegiate sports became evident to me when I agreed to a student request to select a mascot for the UMR campus. The rationale of the students was straightforward. All the other campuses had mascot names. They viewed the mascot as a nickname for the campus. The students wanted to be part of a unique opportunity to select a campus mascot.

The students and the staff designed a process to engage their peers and community members in the selection of a mascot. Per my instructions, they selected three possible mascots for my review. I would select a mascot from the list.

On the day we announced the new UMR mascot to the students and the community, I was overwhelmed by the interest of the local news media and community members attending the announcement. I cannot recall during my ten years at UMR having more interest in an event than the mascot reveal. There seemed to be less interest in the first student move-in and the first graduation. It finally occurred to me following the questions by the media and community members why there was such interest in the mascot reveal. They believed that naming a mascot was the first step toward launching an intercollegiate sports program.

We selected the "raptor" as the UMR mascot. Eventually, the students named the mascot, "Rockie the Raptor." I liked the raptor, a bird of prey, for its excellent vision. I felt that the raptor symbolized UMR's long-term vision. I was the only one who thought this way. Others viewed the raptor as an icon of power and strength. When I reviewed the draft caricatures for the raptor mascot, each captured a very tough and aggressive bird ready to do battle. I wanted a softer image for the raptor mascot. The director of marketing eventually placated me by softening the eyes of the raptor, but otherwise the raptor caricature portrayed an aggressive figure ready to win on the athletic field. Just put on its head a football helmet, pull on a basketball jersey, or put a hockey stick in its hand, Rockie was ready to compete.

After the mascot naming, the conversation restarted about UMR and its intercollegiate sports programs. I again reminded, and again disappointed, many by telling them that operating an intercollegiate sports program was not aligned with campus purpose. The one good outcome was the fun the students had in building the process and selecting and naming their mascot. Otherwise, the ghost got in a good punch. It is an example of a leader who misdirected the investment of mental energy away from campus purpose.

Another category of resource management that directly impacts adaptability and institutional survival are long-term commitments. A leader must think very carefully about making long-term commitments that would restrict future institutional agility. This is especially the case when making a twenty- to thirty-year commitment to a debt service and the maintenance and repair of buildings across their life-span. Such a commitment can restrict agility in the future and compromise institutional survival.

There are many stories in higher education in which the debt service of a campus compromises its credit rating, which then restricts its ability to adapt to the changing landscape of higher education. I discuss more about how to best manage space for a campus with purpose in chapter 5.

The key aspects for being adaptable is deciding how and where to invest your limited assets, both physical resources and mental energy. One must be mindful how resources and mental energies are distributed when designing the structure for a campus with purpose, fully realize the duration of any commitments, and understand how the campus purpose will be perpetuated when making those commitments.

> We must all hang together, or assuredly we shall all hang separately.
> —Ben Franklin

The quote attributed to Ben Franklin reminds me about the power of networks. Networks give the brain its enormous capacity; networks drive the rapid accumulation of new knowledge across the globe; and networks are responsible for the rapid cultural changes observed today. I have learned never to underestimate the power of networks, whether they be neural, digital, or social.

The power of networks and interconnectivity was demonstrated to me in my research on vision. My research team and I spent many years recording the activity of single cells in the brain to better understand how the brain encodes visual information, more specifically, how cells in the brain encode shape, contrast, and movement of visual stimuli. What we and many others realized through our research is that isolated brain cells have a rudimentary capacity to encode information. Stated in a less positive way, I spent years in the lab only to come to the conclusion that individual cells cannot do it by themselves.[14]

Today, we know that the power of the brain is derived from its interconnectivity among a large number of cells. The 100 billion cells in the brain each interconnect on average with 10,000 other cells, creating a large, highly interconnected neural substrate. Interactions among cells in the network make possible the elaborate processing that gives us our exquisite vision. Network models have evolved to explain not only neural processing to support vision and the other senses, but to understand the neural processes underlying many other human capacities, such as learning, memory, and cognition. In parallel, similar network models were developed to explain the interactivity within social systems.

In reading about networks over my research career, I learned that all types of networks exhibit three basic properties: plasticity, density, and hysteresis. Plasticity means that the efficacy of the connections depends on use. Multiple or repeated interactions between two or more units establish new or strengthen existing connections; but if interaction ceases, the connection is weakened and broken. Individuals, like brain cells, must remain jointly interactive or connectivity is lost. So, we can use our connections or lose them. The more two neurons or two people interact, the stronger the connection.

Density is the property of networks where its power is derived, whether it be in its computing capacity or in its impact on culture. Density simply means the greater the number of units and the more the interconnections, the greater the processing power.

The third property is hysteresis, or the stability in dynamic environments. The impact of a single isolated event is diffused and modulated by other activity in the overall network, so there is stability during volatile periods. In dealing with the death of my father, my network of family and friends provided me the stability to adapt to his death and continue with my life. A neural network of the brain reconnects during therapy so an individual partially or fully recovers a function affected by a stroke.

Together, plasticity, density, and hysteresis enable networks to adapt in complex and dynamic environments within the context of its past. The nexus for learning and sustainable change in network models is when new experiences activate a subset of the densely interconnecting existing network that has been shaped by a history of past experiences. Stated differently, the new and the past can "hang together" in the network. The models also demonstrate that when the networks are fragmented and interactivity is low, the networks lose their ability to adapt and self-regulate; and new episodes, regardless of magnitude, are disruptive and the response is unstable. Or in the words of Ben Franklin, we will hang separately.

If this concept is applied to a campus network, its plasticity, density, and hysteresis can serve to balance adaptability and campus purpose. A high degree of interconnectivity within a large campus community network, which includes faculty, staff, students, and community members, increases the likelihood to find common connections between the new and the past, and enhances a capacity to adapt and move forward in a stable, self-regulating, and lasting fashion in response to the volatility of higher education. If we hang together, our interconnectivity enables us to learn as an organization and retain what we have learned, and to do so without sacrificing our commitment to a campus purpose. However, if the campus community network is fragmented, where different factions work independently and compete for resources, the campus network loses its ability to adapt and self-regulate. These properties of networks were central in my thinking about a new structure.

A complex dynamic process involving the interactions between people and ideas exists in adaptive organizations. This interplay between people and ideas must be managed properly by the leader. The demands on a leader in adaptive organizations are much less transactional and much more transformative in nature. Some refer to this as complex leadership, others call it collaborative leadership. Whether you use the expression complex or collaborative, both are based on a perspective about the interactions among people when leading adaptive organizations. Both make the distinction between leaders and leadership. The network is too large, and the interactions are too numerous and complex to be managed by an individual. Complex leadership theory postulates that the central role for a leader is to build leadership capacity within the organization, instilling the habits of interaction to manage the tensions and the products of the interactions.

Lichtenstein et al., in "Complex Leadership Theory: An Interactive Perspective on Leading in Complex Adaptive Systems," states that "Effective organizational change has its own dynamic and that it is subtler and longer than can be managed by a single individual. It is generated by the insights of many people trying to improve the whole, and it accumulates, as it were, over long periods. In other words, leaders in the formal sense can enable the conditions within which the leadership process occurs, but they are not the direct source of the change."[15] Restated using the present terminology, the leader empowers the campus network, optimizes its full density, promotes its plasticity, and gives it time to adapt to change through its hysteresis.

In the next chapters, I will share how I designed the various elements of the structure for a new campus with a purpose embedding these three adaptive properties. With the design of each element of structure, I would ask myself if the administrative and academic model or process empowers students to know and become; if resources and mental energy are channeled on high-yield activities that support campus purpose; and if the way in which the structure is organized and implemented promotes building networks among faculty, staff, students, and community members. Does it leverage the power of the network?

4

Structure with Purpose

Over the next several years, I designed and implemented a structure that supported the UMR campus purpose. I battled with the ghost of university past in order to be free to design better ways to organize ourselves and to do the work of a world class undergraduate health science campus committed as an institution to learn and share what it learns about student learning and development. I incorporated the adaptive planning assumptions in the designs, so the overall structure was agile and empowered faculty and staff to innovate. In this chapter, I describe my thinking, being open to new approaches and mindful of the planning assumptions, about how I approached the design of a specific administrative or academic model or process so it aligned with campus purpose.

Academic Administrative Structure

During my time at the University of Missouri, I was in charge of the review of academic departments and the approval of new degree programs. As I managed the degree program and department inventories, I witnessed degree proliferation, an increase in the number of academic departments, and departmental competition for new degree programs that crossed disciplinary boundaries. This happened during periods when enrollments did not expand in a corollary fashion. Not surprisingly, departmental competition intensified during frequent budget cuts and the ensuing pressure to eliminate academic departments.

As I cogitated about these trends, it became clear that discipline-based academic departments funded by enrollment was not a sustainable practice when student demand and workforce needs are rapidly and constantly shifting during exponential times. To eliminate departmental competition for status and funds, I decided to create only one academic unit to house the faculty and staff. This academic place was to be the home for the campus purpose on learning—the Center for Learning Innovation.

Having only one academic unit that cuts across all academic disciplines is not typical in higher education. The common practice at most established universities is to have many academic departments separated by academic discipline or field of research. This administrative grouping of faculty by academic discipline is linked to the close and deep ties faculty have with their discipline. Some say discipline affiliations are more important to faculty than their campus affiliation, which follows from the plasticity and density properties of social networks.

There is a subculture associated with an academic discipline. Faculty in different academic disciplines are raised differently during their formative years as graduate students and postdoctoral fellows. They encounter distinct ways of thinking, rules of engagement, and mores associated with their academic field of study. At the risk of stereotyping, a chemist will typically engage an issue differently than a philosopher. The housing of faculty from various academic disciplines in the same academic home produces a diverse sociocultural experience for the individual faculty members.

The housing of faculty from different disciplines in the same administrative unit goes against the cultural underpinnings promoted by the ghost. My purpose, however, was to create an academic home that would nurture the formation of a networked community among faculty centered around student learning research and not around an academic discipline. The academic home must be a safe place for faculty and staff to have deep discussions about twenty-first century foundational skills devoid of the customary competition between academic disciplines or between individuals with differing employee status. This would be a place where it was natural for faculty to integrate different ways of thinking associated with the different disciplines to enrich the learning research and curricular conversations.

Deployment of Faculty Talents

As vice president for academic affairs in Missouri, I reviewed tenure policies and wrote new policies for post-tenure review and for nontenure track faculty. I observed that the legacy structure associated with the review for tenure did not fully recognize excellence in teaching and learning, that the mind-set for post-tenure review did not acknowledge the changing role of faculty over their career, and that the current policy for nontenure track faculty was disrespectful.

The tenure review process at many established institutions does not require excellence in teaching and learning. William Massy in his books on reengineering the university described this prevailing habit as "satisficing," which means that we embrace doing just a satisfactory job in our teaching (and this probably goes for service as well), but we demand excellence in research and scholarship.[1]

I encountered this prevailing mind-set about "satisficing" teaching and learning when we launched the New Faculty Teaching Scholars program in Missouri around the year 2000. It was a year-long development program for new faculty during the first three years of their probationary appointment. The program included several overnight retreats and monthly discussion sessions, exposing faculty to new pedagogies, course designs, and learning strategies. The program supported around sixty to eighty new faculty each year.

But here is the rest of the story: I had to fight to launch the faculty development program. Many deans and department chairs, and consequently some chancellors, were not supportive of the New Faculty Teaching Scholars program. They did not want to distract their new faculty with teaching and learning stuff because new faculty needed to focus on their research and securing grants. This was their path to tenure. I never felt this was an either-or proposition—a teacher versus a researcher.

While in Missouri, I again encountered this mind-set about teaching and learning when I examined the overall work of faculty during post-tenure review. Often one observed that the work of many senior faculty shifted from research to providing critical teaching and service duties essential to the functioning of a high-performing academic department. During these reviews of the work by senior faculty, I often heard, "This person would never be tenured here today," implying that their current work focused on teaching and service was not valued.

As I reviewed policies related to nontenure track faculty, I found that faculty not on the tenure track were often described as second-class citizens, even referred to as nonregular faculty—a demeaning term. Clearly, the ghost of university past frowns on nontenure track faculty. With such an explicit mind-set of a class hierarchy, where the value is placed on who said it and not on what was said, it would be difficult to build a highly interactive and productive academic network.

However, I observed leaders of high-performing academic departments who greatly valued the roles played by their nontenure track faculty. A number of department chairs told me that these individuals were the best teachers. They often assigned them to teach the critical feeder courses for their majors. It was not surprising that the high-performing departments in Missouri held a different mind-set and exhibited different habits of interaction to fully engage tenured, tenure track, and nontenure track faculty.

These experiences in Missouri shaped my views about how best to deploy faculty talents in a campus with purpose. I designed a tenure policy at UMR with scholarly work on teaching and learning as the primary area of research, and with work in an academic discipline as a secondary area of research. Consequently, when new faculty were hired, it was clear from the tenure document that their scholarship on teaching and learning was prioritized. The new structure did not incentivize "satisficing."

I also proposed a ten-year probationary period for tenure track faculty. The standard probationary period is six years at most established campuses, with the tenure review occurring during the sixth year. It was often my experience in Missouri that the reviews of a probationary faculty member for tenure during the sixth year were based more on future promise and less on current productivity. This is not surprising given all the complexities today in building a research program. New faculty will build and operate a new laboratory, secure research funding and grants, hire technical staff, connect with and develop new graduate students, launch new courses, and serve on committees for the first time. Six years was simply not long enough to assemble and fund the needed research infrastructure; build the relationships; conduct the research; analyze the results; submit the papers; and have the papers reviewed, rewritten, and accepted for publication, all while teaching classes, advising students, and serving on committees. Although this example primarily describes the world of a new science faculty member, the world of a new faculty member in the humanities is equally onerous. Understandably, tenure review committees focus on progress and promise, and less on achievements and outcomes. I believed that a longer probationary period would benefit both the new faculty member and the institution in its review.

The second reason that I proposed a longer probationary period was that the new UMR faculty member would be switching their area of research from their disciplinary field to student learning and development. It was only fair that a new UMR faculty be given a longer time to make the research transition.

The third reason that I wanted a longer probationary period for new UMR faculty was that their service requirements would be extraordinary. New faculty tend to have lower service responsibilities when housed in departments with senior faculty colleagues at an established campus. The department chair and the senior faculty acknowledge that new faculty should devote more of their time during the early years on teaching and research. Unfortunately, this was not an option when building a new campus with a small number of faculty overall and without any senior faculty colleagues. The new faculty would be required to commit extensive amounts of time serving on faculty and staff search committees, curriculum committees, student conduct committees, and attending to other faculty governance matters.

This pervasive service commitment would hamper the success of the new UMR faculty. The only way that I could imagine to manage their mental energy devoted to necessary and extensive service activities associated with building a new campus, yet have the time to commit to building their new research programs on student learning and development, was to extend the probationary period from six to ten years.

The basic tenets of the proposed UMR tenure policy, the primary area of research being student learning and development and a ten-year probationary period, were reviewed by a system-wide committee of faculty from the other campuses of the University of Minnesota. I met with the group and solicited their support for the proposed tenure policy at UMR. Several faculty members on the committee raised concerns that student learning and development was not a real area of research. The ghost was throwing punches again. Luckily, other members of the faculty committee argued on the grounds of academic freedom that research on student learning and development was a legitimate area of scholarship.

There was agreement among the committee members that a ten-year probationary period was too long. The substance of their counterargument was that having significant time discrepancies for the length of the probationary period across different campuses and colleges would be unfair to new faculty overall. I recommended that they approve an initial ten-year probationary period which would phase out at some future date, when the new campus had a larger faculty cohort and its growth and processes were more stabilized. Otherwise, I argued, it would be unfair to the initial groups of new UMR faculty to overburden them with the necessary service duties associated with building a campus from scratch. The faculty committee was sympathetic and agreed to an eight-year probationary period.

An eight-year probationary period was better than six, but in retrospect I should have pushed harder for ten years. Many new UMR faculty did struggle with the burden of extensive service responsibilities as well as manage a research transition from their disciplinary area to student learning and development. I failed as a leader to properly manage their mental energy. For some new faculty this burdensome workload diluted either their efforts on learning research, on service, or both. It was a maladaptive situation.

During my latter years at UMR, I was very pleased that the president recognized one of the original faculty members at UMR with a systemwide service award for her heroic efforts to build a campus from scratch, both through her outstanding research in student learning and development and through her leadership on service to the campus. Despite the maladaptive situation, several new faculty received tenure at UMR because they were resilient and properly managed their mental energy and time to both build a new campus and develop new research programs on student learning and development. They all deserve awards.

To achieve the campus purpose, my concept was that the tenured and tenure track faculty, whom I referred to as learning-design faculty, designed the learning experience for the student both within their disciplinary cluster but also across the curriculum. This supported their tenure endeavors to meet the criteria for the scholarship of student learning and development.

The nontenure track faculty, whom I referred to as student-based faculty (probably better referred to in the literature today as "professional faculty") implemented the learning experience with a focus on individualized support for students. Their primary role was to interact with students individually or in small groups, both in the classroom and at what we called the Just Ask centers.

The Just Ask centers were spaces distributed throughout the campus that were designed to promote interaction between faculty, especially the student-based faculty, and students. The Just

Ask space adopted different forms and shapes over the years as the number of students increased. The space was designed to accommodate both small groups and individual students. Each space had amenities that enabled students and faculty to write on white walls, project images, or slouch in bean bags. They were designed to be bright, welcoming, and blend in with the remainder of the space. We wanted the Just Ask space to not only be a place you go if you are seeking help, but also a common place that was simply there and where students and faculty hang out.

The Just Ask centers were not tutoring centers. In fact, our early observations found that the students who performed the best in courses tended to frequent and interact at Just Ask. We also discovered that when beginning students first arrived on campus, they held a mind-set that if you are smart, you do not need to seek help. So, student newbies stayed away from Just Ask because they did not want to reveal to others that they were not smart and needed to rely on the interactions with faculty. They quickly overcame this misconception because of the welcoming and social aspects of the Just Ask centers—it was a place to hang out and talk about stuff that was discussed in classes.

The Just Ask centers were popular because of the commitment, camaraderie, and expertise of the student-based faculty. The student-based faculty interacted extensively with many individual students over the course of a semester. As a result, they developed learning relationships with the students. They developed an understanding of the students' strengths and weaknesses. The evolving relationships shaped how the student-based faculty tailored their support for the students. They became academic coaches, pushed when needed, but were supportive and compassionate at other times.

In building learning relationships with the students, the student-based faculty individualized the learning experience. Given the cognitive heterogeneity of students, we can no longer address the learning of all the students in exactly the same way. This was the fundamental contribution of the student-based faculty to student learning at UMR. In surveys, UMR graduates would highly rank the Just Ask centers and their interactions with student-based faculty as one of the reasons they were successful in the rigorous program at UMR.

It is essential to underscore that student-based faculty are not performing the role of graduate teaching assistants. Student-based faculty are credentialed and professional educators. They are not part-time adjuncts, which is an outsourcing practice in our business that is harmful to the continuity of student learning and development. From the outset, I strongly believed that student-based faculty, like learning-design faculty, are full time with a career track defined by peer review, promotions, and salary increases. The main difference is that the student-based faculty did not undergo a full tenure review.

The structure for the deployment of faculty talents and energies enabled the faculty to individualize and customize learning experiences for students, which is a necessity for learning in the twenty-first century. The structure also increased the time and improved the nature of the interactions between faculty and students to enhance the research agenda on student learning and development.

A Foundational and Adaptable Curriculum

When I was in Missouri, its state legislature said that if higher education did not make transfer easy for students, they would legislate a common course numbering system for all public institutions, which had been done in some states. The commissioner of higher education in response to the legislators' concern formed a statewide task force to facilitate transfer of general education courses across two-year and four-year institutions. I was asked to co-chair the task force.

To make a long story short, our task force established a common set of learning outcomes for general education, which we called the Core, while simultaneously respecting campus individuality by encouraging each campus to establish distinctive course pathways to achieve the Core. If students completed the Core at one institution, a block of 42 credit hours transferred, and students were not required by the receiving institution to take any additional courses to fulfill the general education requirement for graduation. On the other hand, if a student transferred prior to completing the Core at one institution, the general education courses taken by the student were subject to a course-by-course evaluation by the receiving institution. The legislature supported the approach, and we fended off at the time any legislation to establish a common course numbering system in Missouri.

The breakthrough for our task force was to place a higher value on the learning resulting from the overall curriculum and not focus on individual, isolated courses. We had to overcome a prevailing habit to focus on "my" course, rather than value "our" curriculum.

When I arrived in Rochester, I avoided using the term general education, since it conjured the idea of a checklist on a menu of isolated courses. Rather, I talked about foundation learning—the outcome of "our" curriculum.

The difference between general education and foundation learning is that the latter is a very prescriptive learning experience intentionally designed to connect and integrate the disciplines using a common set of topics. In our case, health-related topics connected activities across the disciplines. Foundation learning is premised on the assumption that expert learning results from making connections and applying core concepts in new settings.

What foundation knowledge is needed for the twenty-first century? President Aoun in his book made the case that to adapt to a new AI world, every student must have three literacies and four cognitive capacities.[2] The three literacies were technological, data, and human. Technological literacy included knowledge about mathematics, coding, and engineering principles. Data literacy was about the capacity to understand "Big Data" and its analysis using statistics. Human literacy was an understanding about the social situation, so we can communicate and engage with others by leveraging our human capacity.

The four cognitive capacities included critical thinking, systems thinking, entrepreneurship, and cultural agility. Critical thinking was about analyzing ideas skillfully and applying them appropriately. Systems thinking dealt with complexity and the role of context. Entrepreneurship was about the skills to create new jobs and opportunities. Cultural agility was a competency to perform in cross-cultural environments.

As you review Aoun's list in the context of the foundation skills and knowledge needed for the twenty-first century, you might want to revise it by adding, subtracting, or combining the literacies or cognitive capacities. I mention his list to illustrate the tenor of the systemic conversations we must have to better prepare our students for *their* lives and careers.

It was my hope that discussions about foundation knowledge for the twenty-first century were ubiquitous and substantive among faculty and staff in the Center for Learning Innovation. The structure of the Center removed any competition among academic departments for funding through enrollments and prioritized overall student learning and development over learning about an academic discipline. As an example, I heard a physics faculty member in the Center for Learning Innovation state that although he was committed to designing learning experiences in physics so students better understood the principles of physics, he also realized that the most significant and long-lasting impact he had on students was to improve their skills solving complex problems. His research agenda included studying the development of skills to solve complex problem by students in non-physics courses after they had completed a physics course. The nature of this thinking was the product of an academic structure that was aligned with campus purpose: all faculty housed in the Center for Learning Innovation; a tenure policy that prioritized student learning and development; and the foundation property of the curriculum.

There were other advantages of the foundation approach, in which all students had an initial, shared, and integrated learning experience. It was a cohort model. Many students were taking the same courses. Their shared education experience created a sense of belonging and a supporting peer network. Its design underscored for students that foundation knowledge was critical for everyone, so students didn't revise their career aspirations simply to avoid rigorous courses. And it was efficient in its delivery because fewer courses were offered.

The other significant advantage of the foundation approach was that students avoided complicated decisions about selecting general education courses that fulfilled prerequisite requirements for major courses before they really knew their major. A common practice was to assemble an army of academic advisors who spent much of their time guiding first- and second-year students through the morass of individual general education courses to optimize the likelihood that they had completed the prerequisites for possible future major courses. The early educational journey can overwhelm a student with the complexities and ambiguities of the relationship between majors and careers and a perplexing relationship to specific courses. With a foundation approach, the path forward is more direct.

With a foundation approach, the early educational journey focuses on cognitive growth and self-realization. The foundation approach directs the efforts to discover the students' "sweet spot" between strengths and passions, which will better position the student to later choose a career trajectory. This is a critical learning experience for the student in the twenty-first century. Understanding one's passion and one's strengths will be tantamount to successfully navigating a multiplicity of careers that they will experience living during exponential times.

Some argue that a loosely formed general education model permits students to sample a variety of courses which will aid them in determining a career interest. I would argue that we must be more diligent in a discussion about careers with students. It must involve an intentional process for the student to explore their passions and to understand their strengths. The student should work closely with someone who serves the role of a life coach. This individual guides the student to purposefully explore their passion through both educational and life experiences. These experiences are then debriefed within the contexts of related careers and the academic abilities of the student. The process to determine a sweet spot between passion and ability is necessarily continuous and interactive. It requires a much deeper relationship than what typically occurs between an academic advisor and a student in which the main purpose is selecting courses for the next semester. This function of a life coach engaging with students early in their educational journey begins to describe the role of the student success coach, which is covered in greater detail later in the chapter.

Even though I fully embraced a foundation approach for all students, I also knew that I needed to design more flexibility into the later years of the four-year curriculum. Otherwise, the overall curriculum would not be agile and adaptable during exponential times.

This turns into questions about majors. How many? Which ones? I learned from my earlier experience in Missouri that chasing a rapidly shifting landscape of careers during exponential times by generating more and more majors was an unsustainable practice. I decided to initially offer only one degree, the bachelor of science in health sciences. I embedded in the degree requirements a signature capstone experience for all students to build a recurring adaptability into the curriculum. I often used a metaphor of a tree to describe the overall curricular model. The initial years, the foundation learning experience, was the trunk of the tree. The latter years of the curriculum, including the capstone, were the branches of the tree.

My approach in designing the capstone was to recognize in the curricular structure something that I had observed over my administrative career. Student activities and interests reflected in their overall portfolio had a greater impact on their future career than did their major per se. In Missouri, we tracked majors and workers in life science occupations. We found that there were many life science workers with non-biology degrees, (e.g., philosophy, social sciences). Large health information system firms hire many noncomputing and nonengineering graduates to write code. In both cases, the employers were hiring smart and hardworking students, which the students demonstrated by their rigorous coursework and by their portfolio of work. The firms trained the talented and hardworking students to perform the desired tasks.

A signature capstone experience represented by the branches of the tree involved a very deliberate process. The capstone process was intentional about how a student developed it, implemented and experienced it, reflected and wrote about it, and debriefed with advisors about achieving their learning and development objectives. A student, typically in the third year, prepared for the learning experience during the fourth year by writing a capstone proposal reviewed by the faculty. The proposal required the student to consider how they will acquire, integrate, and apply their specific knowledge aligned with their passion—not only the *what*, but also the *why* and the *how*. In the proposal, the student selected an institution for study (not necessarily UMR) and courses. The student must also arrange an internship experience and/or volunteer activities. When taken together, the courses and the external activities created a tailored experiential journey preparing the student for the desired career path, or branch of the tree. The capstone was designed to unbundle the learning and create rich, individualized experiences for all students.

There were other benefits to the capstone. Because of the flexibility afforded by the capstone, students must take ownership for their own learning and preparation—a critical mind-set and skill if they were to be successful during exponential times.

The capstone structure also enabled the student to fully leverage a much larger educational network by tapping into the course offerings at other institutions. For this reason, I often said that the tree curriculum was "pre-everything." Students could take business courses online with another institution to pursue health administration, take art classes at the local community college to pursue prosthetics, complete a minor in public health at the large comprehensive campus to pursue public health careers, or complete a second major in mathematics at a different institution to pursue bioengineering. The capstone structure also deepened the transformational learning of study abroad and study away programs by connecting these experiences with the capstone theme. These are examples and opportunities already pursued and completed by UMR graduates. There are many other stories because all students must complete a signature capstone. The parents of prospective students liked hearing the capstone stories.

Parents were initially skeptical when I first introduced the concept of offering only one degree with a tree structure. Parents of prospective students would ask me what could be done with a bachelor's degree in the health sciences. They asked about the employment listings for health scientists. What is the workforce demand for health scientists? How much does a health scientist make? Parents and many others assumed that a degree was associated with a specific occupation.

I tried to allay parent concerns by stating that their daughters and sons were living during a period when the rate of change is accelerating. We must prepare them differently to thrive in a different world, especially if their son or daughter was interested in a health-related career. I shared with the parents that the curriculum of the bachelor of science in the health sciences embedded health topics in all their courses, so students developed a tacit knowledge about health that was critical for any health occupation—how to think about health issues at both macro and micro levels; how to converse and engage with other health care professionals; and how to approach a health problem. I told them that their daughter or son also developed foundation skills that they needed to navigate through different health career trajectories during periods of rapid change.

My conversations did not typically assuage the concerns of parents. My comments about the curriculum were too futuristic. As a side note, my curricular conversations did resonate with parents who were also educators. We noted that there was a high representation of students whose parents were educators in our early classes. However, most parents wanted more specifics and certainty about future employment and/or graduate/medical school training possibilities for students with a health sciences degree. I had better traction with parents when I described the "pre-everything" aspect of a signature capstone experience.

I reunited with some of the parents four years later when their son or daughter presented their capstone. These culminating presentations by the students were a capstone requirement. Each student introduced their portfolio, which included a section on their passion and career aspirations. They described during their presentation the critical learning and life experiences that they believed prepared them for life and future careers. They included a discussion on the confluence of their passion, strengths, and academic abilities. Some students also talked about their resilience and persistence in confronting personal and academic challenges.

The capstone presentations were well attended by faculty, fellow students, and mentors who had developed relationships with the students during their research, clinical, or volunteer experiences of their capstone. It was not unusual for parents and family members to also attend. I attended all that my schedule permitted. The capstone presentations were excellent summations about knowing and becoming. In fact, we began to videotape the presentations to provide us data that we could use to monitor the impact of the curriculum.

The student capstone stories were personal and inspiring. The parents were so grateful to witness the cognitive development and maturation of their sons and daughters over the past four years. The faculty and staff also felt like proud parents. Tissues were required!

For me, the capstone presentations reminded me about why I was in the business of developing human potential. I observed the power of the network—faculty, staff, community mentors, and fellow students—supporting the students to live their passion. I saw a curriculum enable students to know and become. I observed soon-to-be graduates who weren't wedded to a specific job or occupation, but understood their own passion, abilities, and strengths, and embraced change as part of life's journey. The capstones demonstrated to me that UMR had prepared students for their lives and careers. Many parents concurred. Maybe this is why I received as many hugs from parents as graduates after commencement.

But during the launch of the new curricular structure, I often felt that the ghost of university past was speaking through the parents, like a ventriloquism act. The ghost of the university past does not support the concept that students can study at different institutions of higher education during the capstone. The ghost embraces autonomy and a do-it-on-your-own mentality. The ghost promulgates that many majors are needed to address varying student interests, not a capstone. The ghost does not embrace the lack of focus on a specific academic discipline. What the ghost dislikes the most is a learning focus on the curriculum and student experiences and not on the individual course.

This concern that an individual course is not fundamental to student learning was made evident to me during a question session after a presentation that I made at a conference. After describing the foundational and adaptable aspects of the tree curricular model, a non-UMR faculty member stated that the structure violated the academic freedom rights of the faculty. She said the model prescribed what faculty should teach. She and I had different definitions of academic freedom. Faculty working together to integrate and connect learning experiences across courses around health topics was not a breach of academic freedom. Nonetheless, I followed up on her comment in an attempt to better understand what was underneath her concern.

Following our discussion, I concluded that her comment revealed more about a prevailing mind-set about autonomy and independence than concerns about academic freedom. Faculty are hired and supported as independent knowledge contractors. The prevailing habit is to focus on individual faculty. So faculty are conditioned to work individually and independently. Maybe this is why in part we count multi-authored research papers differently than single-authored papers in a tenure review, or teaching load is counted differently when a course is team taught versus taught by one person.

However, faculty must work together in order to leverage the power of a network to nurture and sustain the campus purpose. A faculty network introduces new interdependencies. Faculty who are part of a team designing a foundation curriculum must rely on each other to cover certain material connected with a specific concept at a particular time to achieve the integrated goals of the curriculum.

In contrast, faculty teaching at most established institutions have fewer constraints. The faculty member must teach the assigned course during the time the course is scheduled and at a place where it is scheduled. Otherwise, the design and the coverage of the material in the course is completely at the discretion of the faculty member.

A new set of interdependencies is embedded in the design of the foundation curriculum. Some faculty view the interdependencies as restrictive and burdensome. Again, this is a testament to the faculty at UMR who learned to manage these interdependencies and put in the extra effort to work collaboratively with their faculty colleagues to build a learning experience that better prepares students for their lives and careers.

As an example of the extra effort put into managing the interdependencies in building a foundation curriculum, Claudia Neuhauser, the first vice chancellor for academic affairs at UMR, worked closely with the new faculty and the IT staff to build and launch intelligent System for Educational Assessment of Learning (iSEAL). iSEAL was a curriculum management tool designed to purposefully manage the interdependencies of faculty teaching different courses in an integrated curriculum. To the best of our knowledge at the time, there were no curriculum learning systems available. All the learning systems that were on the market, and the one implemented at the University of Minnesota, were course-based. The ghost had a stronghold on how learning system companies provided technical support.

As the faculty were building an integrated curriculum, they agreed to tag different learning concepts and objects which were part of their courses with specific learning outcomes. A learning object is a grouping of course-specific content and the concepts linked with the content along with the student practice and products associated with the content, including an assessment of the student's work. As an example, consider a learning object on health disparity prepared by a faculty member teaching in a public health course. The faculty member designed exercises and projects for the students to identify factors underlying health disparities, sort through national health databases by race and ethnicity to identify differences in health status, read and analyze papers on prevention, and so on. The products of the students' work and their assessments, written tests, essays, and group projects were tagged with the overall and specific learning objectives of the curriculum under knowledge in the health sciences, intellectual and practical skills, self-regulation, and social engagement.

iSEAL was the tool that enabled the faculty to tag the students' work and store the work in a common repository to be analyzed later. UMR implemented a student computer program. Each student was provided a computer that was equipped with iSEAL. All students completed their course work using the iSEAL system. In this way, all student work was tagged and stored.

The major benefit of iSEAL was that it provided a rubric for faculty to connect student work in their individual courses to the learning goals and objectives for the entire curriculum. iSEAL also provided information about the coverage and the distribution of specific learning objectives across the curriculum. The faculty could then ask, Did we provide sufficient coverage of topics in our courses to develop student diversity awareness and intercultural competency, quantitative reasoning, critical thinking, and so forth?

All of us dreamed about studying the stored and tagged student work to measure the development of skills and concepts associated with the different learning objectives as the students progressed through the curriculum. The faculty could ask, Does the student gain more quantitative reasoning skills as they encounter more quantitative tasks in the curriculum? Do they develop better complex problem-solving skills as they progress through the curriculum? Do students who struggle with a specific concept in biology also struggle with another concept in chemistry? If so, can we use this correlation to intercede and better support student success?

Instead of just looking at the student's grade in a course in statistics taken during the first year, the faculty had a better assessment of the statistical aptitude of a student if they analyzed the entire portfolio of student work across the curriculum, where they encountered in subsequent courses more statistical concepts and performed more statistical tests. A measure based on a curricular experience would be more valid and informative than a grade based solely on a single course experience.

During my time at UMR, my dream was that we would develop a student record that emulated a medical record. To better understand student learning and development, we need much more information than that provided by a student transcript, which is just listing courses and grades. However, the faculty and IT staff never quite unraveled all the challenges associated with a systemic rubric-based analysis of a student's portfolio of work stored in iSEAL. It turned out to be more of a data science issue, which we were not adept at solving by ourselves.

Today, UMR is no longer implementing the home-grown iSEAL system. Other learning systems have evolved and are supported by the University of Minnesota system that can be used by UMR faculty to continue the focus on curriculum-based learning by tagging and storing student work in a format that is analyzable. The UMR faculty learn by doing. I am confident that in the near future, with the right data science expertise, they will fully reap the benefits focusing on the curriculum and not just a single course. In doing so, they will continue to fulfill the campus purpose by conducting world class, distinctive, and value-added research on student learning and development.[3]

About three years after we launched the bachelor of science in health sciences degree program, we added a second major, the bachelor of science in health professions. The second degree program did not include a capstone since the pathway followed by the student needed to be more prescriptive. The students entered this program during their third year after completing the foundation curriculum for their first two years. In this degree program, the student was completing both certification requirements for practicing in an allied health field, such as respiratory care, radiography, sonography, and echocardiography, while completing their work for a baccalaureate degree in the health professions. All the allied health fields shared the same baccalaureate degree in the health professions, but the clinical certifications differed.

This second degree program was offered in collaboration with The Mayo Clinic School of Health Sciences. It conformed to the campus purpose. The second degree program had a distinctive curricular design involving a unique partnership between two educational entities. It was designed to ratchet up the critical thinking and analytical skills that would be required to address the greater complexity associated with the future practice in these clinical fields. It was world class because it involved a partnership with a world class organization involving training in world class facilities with world class equipment. It also added value for both the student and the City for Health. At the time of this writing, 100 percent of the graduates of the bachelor of science in health professions passed certification exams and were employed in the allied health fields supported by the program. Many of the graduates are currently employed in Rochester.

The tree structure of the curricular model is foundational, customizable, affordable, and adaptable. It has the agility to address a shifting set of learning experiences that will be demanded by the ever-changing workforce of the twenty-first century. It is aligned with campus purpose. It is distinctive, world class, and adds values to the students, higher education institutions, and to the health care workforce of the region.

Nearly all the UMR graduates pursued health-related careers following graduation. About a third of the graduates were accepted and attended a medical school or a graduate program in a health-related field. Another third of them were employed in health-related jobs, many in the allied health fields. And the final third decided to take a bridge year. These graduates continued their clinical or research experiences following graduation to bolster their competitiveness for admission into clinical or graduate programs. They also used this time to learn more about themselves and their passion before embarking on their next educational journey.

I was thrilled by the success of UMR graduates. The students discovered career trajectories that were aligned with their sweet spot between passion and abilities. The need for a health care workforce covers a full spectrum, from patient-based to non-patient-based services, from primary to secondary and tertiary care, from research to the bedside, from health policy to social work, from the management of disease to the management of wellness, from physical health to mental health, and from health care practitioner to administrator. UMR graduates pursued all these areas.

I discovered, though, that the ghost measures the success of an undergraduate experience in the health sciences by the percentage of graduates who are accepted into medical school. Nearly half of the UMR students during their first year expressed a desire to attend medical school. Many parents of prospective students wanted their son or daughter to become a doctor. However, only 5–10 percent of UMR graduates eventually pursued and attended medical school even though the acceptance rate of UMR students who did apply to medical school was above the national average.

Over the course of the student's journey at UMR, they learned by observation and experience what it means to be a medical doctor and what it takes to be a medical doctor. Many students discovered that "being a doctor" wasn't aligned with their passion. Other students learned that they did not have the academic abilities to be admitted into a medical school. However, they all learned the plethora of ways that they can live their passion to care for others. This student experience was the primary construct that undergirded the design of the foundation and customizable degree program. Its structure supported the student's discovery of passion and abilities and their alignment with a career trajectory.

The real measure of success of the tree curricular structure will be if UMR graduates can adapt and thrive during exponential times. UMR will simply need to stay in close contact with graduates to assess how well the curricular structure prepared them for their lives and careers and how the curricular structure can be revised to do it better. This should be the purpose of the emerging UMR alumni program—focus on preparedness, not just on fundraising, during exponential times.

Pedagogy

Around the year 2000, I was fortunate to join a board of a state-wide organization committed to reform K-12 education with new teaching and learning strategies. The program was called electronic Missouri Innovative Teaching Strategies (eMINTS).

As part of my board duties, I toured the innovative classrooms across the state. On my first visit, I was struck by the noise and chaos in the eMINTS classroom, which was the opposite of my concept of a well-managed classroom with students working diligently and quietly at their desks. This was my first introduction to a student-centered, rather than a teacher-centered classroom, where the students working in teams are actively engaged on projects using digital tools.

I was amazed by the student excitement about their projects and their time on task. I was also impressed by the improvement not only in state test scores for all students who participated in these classrooms, but also impressed by how this pedagogy reduced the test score disparity between students of color and their peers.

The teachers in these classrooms preached to me about rigor, relevance, and relationships. They said that the teacher must demand rigor, and the students will raise the quality of their work to meet your expectations. They talked about the importance of engaging student interests by choosing relevant topics to guide their learning about core skills. If students were interested in airplanes, use airplanes to help them learn math and spelling. And finally, the teachers underscored the value of relationships among their peers. Students simply work harder to please their peers than to please their teachers.

As I prepared to leave Missouri for Minnesota, the leadership of the eMINTS project hosted a farewell lunch. It was there that I shared with them that I wanted to start the first eMINTS university.

To lay the groundwork for this pedagogical approach in Rochester, I immediately equipped all the classroom space with furniture that was designed to support student-centered instruction. I only hired faculty if they embraced the concept of a student-centered pedagogy, understanding that each would differ in how they would implement their student-centered approach. I preached to faculty and staff about the importance of engaging our students with health-related topics, encouraging team-based, project-based work, and to holding the students to high standards.

We prepared our new incoming students for student-centered instruction. I described the three Rs of UMR—rigor, relevance, and relationships—to prospective students and their families during visit days. The visit days included a learning experience that was multidisciplinary and student-centered. Finally, we never used the term "classrooms." We referred to these spaces during campus tours as "Learning Labs." It was our intent that by using the term Learning Lab, students, when entering these spaces, would bring a new active mind-set about their role in learning and no longer expect the faculty to spend the next fifty minutes lecturing to them.

This form of pedagogy conformed to the planning assumption about leveraging the power of networks. It required the faculty to develop ways for students in all courses across the curriculum to learn how to work with each other. Teamwork in some form is a foundation skill of the twenty-first century. When we admitted our first first-year class in fall 2009, student-centered instruction was considered new and innovative. However, having all courses, not just some, offered in this format created a clear identity for UMR—an institution committed to innovation in student learning and development.

There were concerns when we first launched the student-centered pedagogy, flipped classrooms, and students working as teams. First-year students complained that they were put in groups to do classwork, but they did not know how to work in teams. I remember one of the students in our first class sharing with me that she did not want to work on a team. "I want to get into medical school. Why would I share what I know with other students? I will be competing against them to get into medical school." With a little coaching, the students learned quickly and became very competent working in teams. It was impressive to observe sophomores and juniors work together in teams when given a group task. They quickly analyzed the task at hand; assigned different tasks according to the strengths of different team members; designated someone to coordinate the overall project, which included managing team members' schedules; and often they would design some form of quality control.

I remember a student telling me about her interview for admission into a medical school. She was asked if she could describe a time when she worked as part of a team. She told the interviewer that teamwork was something she did every day at UMR. She then told the interviewer that she had learned from her experiences at UMR how to form good teams, how to be a good team player, and how to deal with conflicts and struggles when working on a team.

Some were concerned about freeloaders on teams. Several faculty attempted to assess freeloading by asking each student to rate the contribution of the other members of the team. They found no evidence of systemic freeloading, especially when every team member had a specific task.[4]

Others were concerned that shy students or less socially skilled students would be disadvantaged by teamwork assignments. A UMR faculty member in sociology measured social efficacy of students and found that students with low social efficacy performed as well as their peers on team-based projects.[5]

Another faculty member demonstrated the value of working in teams as a tool to enhance student learning. The faculty member administered tests twice. The first time the students took the test individually. Then the faculty member administered the same test a second time, but this time the students prepared their answers working in their group. A student improved her grade several percentage points if the team performed better on the group test than the student did on the individual test, which typically was the case.

As the faculty member listened to the group conversations, he did *not* hear "What was your answer on number 4? Oh, I had a different answer. What was your answer on number 5? And so on." He also noted that students did not simply use the recognized smart student's answers. Rather, he was more likely to hear: "What was your answer on number 4? Oh, I had a different answer. Why did you answer this way? I didn't think about that. It makes sense to me now." And the teams prepared their answer through debate and not simply entrusting that the smart student always had the correct answer. The team tests were rich learning experiences for the students. Students teach and learn from each other. It is the power of the network.

UMR faculty who had previously taught at other institutions often commented that they did not have to manage absenteeism any longer. The students working in teams held each other accountable for their attendance, which increased overall time on task.

One final story is not about teamwork but more about the general philosophy of student-centered learning. I was walking behind two first-year students one morning. They did not know that I was behind them. The one student said to the other, "I don't know why they pay Professor X, she doesn't teach us anything. She makes us learn it on our own." The students then noticed that I was behind them and looked at me with embarrassment. I told them to hang in there, and I assured them that Professor X was working really hard to create a guided learning experience so "you do learn it on your own. That is her purpose." At the end of the semester, I again encountered these two students. They shared with me that they liked the course and learned a lot. In high school, they were simply accustomed to being fed information via a lecture. They would memorize the highlights of the lecture material organized on a study sheet prepared by the teacher. Then they would take a test. At UMR, they said, they had to learn the material by understanding it.

Some will always be concerned, especially the ghost, that I overstepped my bounds as an administrator by pushing a common pedagogical approach. I do not regret my decision and it was perfectly aligned with campus purpose.

Integrating Academic and Student Affairs

At the University of Missouri, I supported the chair of the academic and student affairs committee of the board of curators. The agenda for this board committee was typically dominated by academic matters, such as new degree programs, tenure policies, or research funding. There were periodic presentations by the student affairs staff, much of it dealing with student conduct issues, fraternity behavior, and student fees. This was the pattern for many years, until one year, a new board member chaired the committee. She wanted to devote the agenda to student affairs.

Her emphasis on student affairs created a transformative learning experience for me. I had the pleasure to closely work with four stellar student affairs leaders over the course of the year. I learned that student affairs was much more than clubs, student recreation centers, and student discipline. They also shared with me that they felt their important work was not viewed as academic and hence not valued on their campuses, another inherited mind-set promoted by the ghost of university past.

Being mindful of my planning assumption that learning today was about knowing and becoming, I called my student affairs colleagues in Missouri and asked them how to raise the status of student affairs when building a new campus. They suggested that I create a student affairs unit that directly reported to me, the chancellor, rather than to the provost or vice chancellor for academic affairs. I followed their recommendation, but it was a mistake. With separate reporting lines, the academic and student affairs units became siloed, and the faculty and staff in the two units were not working together in ways that I had hoped or imagined.

In retrospect, I asked the wrong question of the student affairs leaders. Rather than ask about status, I should have asked "How does an institution best support both student learning and development?" I know today that the answer was less about an organizational structure and more about institutional culture—fighting the ghost of university past. It was about creating an institutional mind-set that developing human potential is about knowing and becoming. It was about nurturing an active network of faculty, student development staff, and students. And it was also about assembling the right leadership who championed the critical connection between academic affairs and student development.

The key talent in our effort to support "becoming" was embodied in the position of a student success coach.[6] Because the design of the first two years of curriculum was prescriptive with limited course choices, UMR did not need an academic advisor to focus on assisting students to navigate the confusion surrounding general education courses. UMR needed someone who had the time, resources, and skills to develop a "becoming" relationship with each student. I wanted someone who could be the safe harbor for a student to discuss her dreams, her fears, her personal challenges, her academic concerns, and her uncertainties. As this relationship is formed and deepened over the course of the first year, it must be continued and leveraged over the next three years as the student faces new challenges, recovers from new mistakes, makes new decisions, and prepares for life after graduation. As we talked about the three Rs at UMR, the most important "*Relationship*" was the one manifested by the special bond formed between the student and the student success coach.

The student success coach was a combination of academic advisor, counselor, and life coach. The student success coaches were essential in guiding students to discover their sweet spot between passion and ability. They assisted students in finding volunteer opportunities or other experiences to search for activities that aligned with their passion. They debriefed with the students about their academic performance in the context of their imagined careers. The student success coaches often had the first conversation with a student, who had dreamed of going to medical school ever since kindergarten, that attending medical school was unlikely. The student success coaches shared in the sorrow but then redirected the student to consider other ways that aligned with their abilities to live their passion to care for others. The student success coaches counseled students how to structure a conversation with their parents that going to medical school was their parent's dream and not theirs. They wanted to pursue a different career trajectory to care for others. The student success coaches were often first to know if students were struggling physically or mentally and referred students to the appropriate support services.

All of this was a lot to ask from a student success coach. As a leader, I needed to properly manage their mental energy so they developed and supported the "becoming" relationships with students. To do this, I battled with the ghost. The prevailing habit in higher education was to assign one academic advisor to about 200 to 300 students. New academic advisors were often assigned as the student progressed from their first year to their senior year. Many initially thought that the new position of a student success coach was similar to an academic advisor.

Hence budget and human resource officers argued that we needed to hire just two or three student success coaches to accommodate the 400 to 600 students that were enrolled at UMR. I knew that a ratio of 200 to 300 students to one coach certainly diluted if not undercut the purpose of the position of the student success coach. I argued strongly for much lower ratios—50 students to one coach. We eventually settled on a ratio of 75 students to one coach during the first year, but with student attrition that ratio was near 50 to one during the student's senior year.

Some argued that UMR was inefficient because it deployed a lower ratio of students to coaches. I ignored the ghost. The student success coach fulfilled a different role than an academic advisor. They were absolutely critical if we adhered to the design principle that learning is about knowing and becoming. This was an investment with immense returns on student success. I witnessed it each year at the chancellor's reception prior to commencement. The students gathered around their student success coach and reminisced about their "becoming" during their time at UMR.

The student success coaches also participated in delivering a student development part of the curriculum. At most established institutions, a freshmen seminar was offered for students in their first semester. These seminars typically met once a week for about an hour and the topics include time management skills, social opportunities, and support services. The freshmen seminar was mainly an orientation to the campus with some support to deal with the transition between high school and college.

At UMR, the student success coaches offered a similar orientation and time management course that met once a week during the first semester. However, they also administered Strength Finder, the Intercultural Development Inventory, and the ACT Engage. The coaches then discussed with the students the overall results in class, but also debriefed students about their individual results during their private meetings. They readministered the surveys at several points throughout the four-year curriculum. These pre- and post-measures enabled the student success coaches to track student development as the students matured and grew with new experiences.

These pre- and post-measures also enabled faculty and staff to assess the impact of the curricular design on student development in areas of cultural competency, management of strengths and weakness, and changes in psychosocial attributes. Because diversity awareness and intercultural competency were considered a foundation learning outcome and embedded throughout the curriculum, the Intercultural Development Inventory, which provided a common language and metric for intercultural competency, enabled the faculty and student development staff to measure the achievement of that learning outcome across all four years of the curriculum.

The student development portion of the curriculum was not just offered as a freshmen experience, but across all four years at UMR. Other student development seminars included topics such as eating healthy, living on purpose, stress inoculation and management, preparation for standardized tests (MCATS and GREs), preparing the capstone proposal, writing the summative capstone portfolio, and preparing for the capstone presentation.

Eventually and despite my false start, an active network of faculty, student success coaches, and other student support staff emerged at UMR and blended together their talents to interweave knowing and becoming. They all worked jointly to identify student strengths, support a student's exploration of passion, and create pathways for academic and life success. They created intentional experiences embedded into the curriculum for all students, from the first year through the capstone, focused on student development.

The network of faculty and student development staff also developed a set of institutional student development outcomes by debating, prioritizing, refining, and exploring outcome measures. They partnered on research examining the interplay across instructional models, academic success, and student psychosocial attributes; and they implanted into the curriculum community engagement experiences for all students. They designed a model so community-based projects were sustainable, benefiting both community partners and students, and served as a tool to achieve student learning and development outcomes.

The UMR model for community and civic engagement became known as Community Collaboratory (Co-Lab). In Co-Lab, UMR formed a partnership with a community-based organization. A faculty member and a representative of a community organization were assigned to supervise a group of typically five to seven students for a semester. The students, working with the community partner, designed a project, implemented it, wrote a report, and presented it to a wider audience of faculty and community partners. The students were instructed to not only summarize and analyze their progress over the course of the semester, but also to recommend the next steps to a new group of students to build on their progress during the following semester. The purpose of this feature in the design of Co-Lab was to provide continuity of the project across semesters, which delivered more value to the community partners.

As an example, the Salvation Army in Rochester was a community partner for the Co-Lab course. At the request of the representative of the Salvation Army, UMR students were asked to work with immigrants to prepare them to take GED exams. The first group of students designed an approach to work as a team to tutor and prepare immigrants for the GED exam. At the end of the semester, the students concluded that the most significant barrier for local immigrants taking the GED exam was their lack of computer skills. It turned out that the GED exams were administered with computers. The following semester, a second group of students picked up the project from the first group and began to design a training program to develop the computer skills of local immigrants. At the end of their semester, the second group of students discovered that the Salvation Army was not equipped with a sufficient number of modern computers to meet the demand for the training program designed and offered by the UMR students. The students recommended in their report that the next group consider ways to secure access to additional and newer computers. The third group of students started their project examining different options to secure additional computers to be housed in the Salvation Army facility. They wrote a grant to a local community foundation. The grant was approved, and the Salvation Army was awarded funding to purchase new computers. The fourth group of students helped set up the computers and delivered the training program. They recommended in their report ways to lessen staff demands and improve the training program. The fifth group of students conducted an assessment of the computer training program and recommended revisions. And I suspect that some form of this project with the Salvation Army continues today.

The distinct advantage of the design of Co-Lab was its continuity across semesters and across groups of students. The community partners saw real value for their organization being part of Co-Lab. The community partner representative became adept working with different groups of students over several semesters. They learned when to push, when to advise, or when to sit back and let the students struggle with the complexity of the project. The community organization representatives were as concerned as the faculty that Co-Lab was a learning experience for the students. The students learned about project management, working in teams, and about "wicked problems."[7] When I listened to the end of the semester Co-Lab presentations, it was clear that the community and civic engagement experience was a "becoming" experience for the students.

Co-Lab was a requirement for every UMR student. I was initially worried that we would not be able to scale up the Co-Lab program to serve all our students. As word about the design and success of Co-Lab spread across community and civic organizations, we had little problem recruiting and working with an ample number and variety of community partners.

The development of Co-Lab was one approach to leverage the assets of the City for Health. Another approach that connected students with the City for Health was the capstone. Many students in their capstone projects spent considerable time working in research laboratories, working in the Center for Innovation at the Mayo Clinic, working as medical scribes, helping administer clinical research projects, and supporting other civic and clinical opportunities that resided in Rochester.

UMR also expanded its work study programs by developing relationships with nonprofits so students could work in the City for Health as well as work at UMR. This was a great opportunity for students who qualified for this federal student aid, which provided a significant financial benefit for the nonprofit organizations since eighty cents of every dollar of the student's salary was covered by the federal work study program.

There were many other unstructured ways that UMR students connected with the City for Health. Many UMR students volunteered at the Mayo Clinic and other health care facilities in Rochester. Students volunteered at the Ronald McDonald House, a hospice facility, a place that housed individuals awaiting a transplant, county office of public health, and an elder care facility.

One of my favorite stories about a volunteer opportunity for students was hand massages. The students provided hand massages to patients awaiting a stressful treatment, such radiation or chemotherapy. The purpose of the hand massage was to relax the patient before the procedure. Just imagine walking up to a stranger in a waiting room who is dealing with a serious illness and asking them if you can give them a hand massage, chatting with them during the massage. This was certainly a "becoming" experience for the students, especially for students whose passion was patient care.

Another favorite was music by the bedside. Students with musical talents volunteered for a program at Mayo Clinic which arranged musical visits to patient rooms as a means to relax, entertain, and brighten the day of patients in the hospitals. The student musicians often played guitar and sang. This was another great "becoming" experience for the students.

As a result of these structured and unstructured engagements with the communities in the City for Health, many students developed mentor relationships with health care clinicians, administrators, researchers, and leaders of community organizations. It would be difficult to discern today which of all these interactions, whether they were with a student success coach, a faculty member, or a community leader, were under the purview of academic affairs or student development. That was a good sign. The blending of academic affairs and student development was aligned with campus purpose and mindful that today and in the future student learning was about knowing and becoming. It was another thread of the campus purpose for an undergraduate program in the health sciences that was distinctive, world class, and value added.

5

Buildings versus Space

When I use the expression, building a campus from scratch, many believe that I am referring to the construction of buildings. We associate a campus with its infrastructure. If I ask an alumnus to show me a picture of their university, they select a photograph that highlights the campus buildings, and maybe some students and faculty can be seen in the background. Rarely the alumnus selects a picture that centers on the students, faculty, or staff with buildings in the background.

I leave board meetings with the same impression that universities are about buildings. The board agenda is dominated by topics related to the campus infrastructure, such as procuring land, demolishing buildings, operating power plants, running water, steam, and electrical lines, designing new buildings, bidding construction contracts, constructing new buildings, and operating and maintaining the capital infrastructure. It is not surprising that academic topics are dwarfed at board meetings given the complexity and enormity of operating your own "little city." I worried that all the complexity associated with a "little city" being the campus misdirected mental energy and physical resources away from fulfilling the campus purpose.

I am reminded of the quote attributed to Darwin in the planning assumption. Putting the quote in the present context, "It is not the campus that has the greatest number or the largest buildings that will survive, but the campus that is the most adaptable to change will survive." I have concluded that a large infrastructure hampers the adaptability of a campus during exponential times.

I learned that 20 percent or less, depending on how it was calculated, of the total cost of a building was related to its construction. The other 80 percent were costs associated with the operation, including utility and personnel costs, and maintenance of the building over its lifetime.[1] To illustrate the consequences of this distribution of the overall costs of a building, when a board secured $50 million from a donor or from the state to construct a new building, they were also committing to pay additional $200 million over the life-span of the building to cover its operation and maintenance.

Neither states nor donors have the proclivity to provide new financial support to cover the recurring costs for the operation and maintenance of new buildings, which means these new costs were absorbed by normal operating revenues generated by state funding and tuition. Given the direction of state funding, student tuition was increasingly picking up more of this tab. In this scenario, resources, especially those generated by student tuition, are diverted away from making investments in an undergraduate program in the health sciences and in research on student learning and development. Building a little city for the UMR campus compromised its purpose to be world class, distinctive, and value added.

I also learned that the distribution of space in the "little cities" as campuses does not conform to the campus purpose. Space utilization studies typically show that a small fraction of the available space is actually used for undergraduate instruction. Most of the space is devoted to faculty and administration offices and for research laboratories.

Finally, a prevailing habit of higher education was to build buildings to last a long time. A downside of this habit was that the space in existing buildings was often not designed to meet current needs. Imagine the difficulty and cost to reconfigure a large, tiered classroom into a student-centered classroom. The rigidity of antiquated infrastructure drives even more new construction in order to meet today's functional space needs. There was also a hesitancy to demolish older buildings, often for historical reasons. Unfortunately, this pattern of keeping the old and adding new has expanded the overall campus footprint, which further exacerbates mounting operation and maintenance bills. The rising building costs divert resources away from investing in the campus purpose and stifle a campus's agility to adapt.

Add to this escalating cost cycle a common practice to defer building maintenance, especially during lean fiscal periods. Some argue that for each dollar of maintenance deferred today will cost you three to four dollars tomorrow.[2] This creates a maintenance and repair crisis that overwhelms campus resources and mental energy.

Once you understand the available revenue sources that covered these swelling operation and maintenance costs, and that student tuition covered a disproportionate share of these costs, it becomes clear that students are needed to pay for the buildings. I wanted to invest resources generated by student tuition on programs that were world class, distinctive, and value added.

This skewed behavior was consonant with our custom to associate campuses with buildings and not with people, which also explained a fascination with new buildings. I encountered this fascination with having shiny new buildings during my listening and welcoming tour. The first questions asked by community members were rarely about students, faculty, or staff, but about dorms, a student center, or a hockey arena.

Campuses are about people, and not about buildings. As a chancellor of a campus with purpose, I wanted to attend to the learning business rather than the real estate business. I wanted buildings to serve students and not the reverse. My approach was to understand space needs and not dwell on new buildings. Space can be part of one building, distributed across several buildings, shared with others, and be temporary.

What are the properties about space that best support the campus purpose? I found answers to this question in the planning assumptions. First, space must support the creation of living and learning communities—leverage the power of networks. Space must be designed to connect faculty and students. Space must connect the students. Space must connect the faculty. Space must also be embedded in and connected with the external health care community.

Second, the space must be flexible and adaptable. I cannot tell you today how many bricks nor how much mortar we will need in ten years to provide the space to support new emerging pedagogies. To preserve institutional agility and its future adaptability, I did not commit to a space arrangement for an overly long time period.

Thirdly, I wanted the institution's mental energy to be devoted to student learning and development in the health sciences and not be misdirected and dominated by the operation and maintenance of the space. This is why I aggressively pursued public-private partnerships.[3,4]

UMR entered into several public-private partnerships to address space needs. One partnership involved the construction and operation of a $30 million building. It was a mixed-use facility, and UMR had a time-limited lease for 80 percent of the building. The space included dorm rooms, office space for faculty and staff, faculty and student interactive spaces, and learning labs. In these private-public partnerships, we focused on what we do best—the learning and development of students. The private entity focused on what it does best—designing, building, managing, maintaining, and operating the building. Public-private partnerships are emerging as a new approach to manage space in higher education. Evidence is beginning to accumulate showing that space cost is less in a private-public partnership than owning and operating the building separately. Nevertheless, the fact that UMR does not own any buildings is another reason why some believe that UMR is not a "real university."

The ghost put up a tough fight to prevent the creation of public-private partnerships at UMR. Remember the ghost believes in autonomy—a do-it-on-your-own mentality. However, also embedded in this do-it-on-your-own mentality is the notion that "we do it better" and "we can't trust others to do it as well." Given this prevailing mind-set, it was difficult to even begin a conversation with senior leaders about a public-private partnership for the $30 million building.

When working with a partner, it is necessary to acknowledge that all parties yield some control and tolerate some ambiguity. Partnerships are formed when the partners believe that the benefits of working together far exceed the inconvenience of losing some control and dealing with some ambiguity. This aspect of working with partners from the private sector can be an impassable cultural hurdle for many in higher education.

For me the benefit of creating a public-private partnership was that UMR was out of the real estate business, expending its mental energy and investing its financial resources to achieve the campus purpose. What drove my thinking about space is that campuses are fundamentally about people and their work—not about buildings.

6
Building and Flying the Plane at the Same Time

The start-up planning (concept and design) that I described in the previous chapters occurred mainly between 2007 and 2009. We admitted our first group of students, who I affectionately called the "trailblazers," in the fall of 2009. During the next five years, the faculty, staff, students, and I often felt that we were building and flying the plane at the same time.

When I reflect back on those middle years during my tenure at UMR, it was a difficult and challenging period. The tensions were not solely over campus purpose or the design of the structure. Rather, one source of tension was related to managing a visceral expectation that UMR would expand. I didn't want the plane to be overloaded. The other source of tension was related to constantly making decisions about critical operational minutia to keep the plane in flight.

To curtail a mind-set that bigger is better, I learned the art of saying no. I needed to properly channel mental energy and invest limited physical resources to conform to the campus purpose. As I mentioned previously, we as leaders of established campuses have created expansive expectations. Faculty, staff, students, and stakeholders are not hesitant to request the involvement of the campus in entertainment, community development, political endeavors, business development, and other well-intentioned activities.

The daily routine of a campus leader includes meeting with stakeholders, faculty, staff, and students listening to their requests for funding or programmatic support for exciting, well-reasoned, and impactful initiatives. As a leader you cannot support every new idea or initiative that comes through your office door, but at the same time, you do not want to dampen innovative energy and community enthusiasm. Developing an artful way to say no was critical to balancing these tensions.

A strategic plan by directing resource allocations should provide a rationale for saying no. If the plan is vague and embraces a nonprioritized broad scope of activities, which many do, the plan lacks a reason for a leader to say no. A plan with clear tactics, funding streams identified, and a time frame arms a leader to say no to any requests for investments outside the plan parameters.

Conversely, an overly tactical and rigid plan may be detrimental to a campus that needs to adapt during exponential times. A five-year plan today may feel like eternity when new ideas not in the original plan are needed to accommodate the rapid changes in higher education.

I have experienced the downsides of broad, nonspecific, and rigid tactical plans. This was one reason why I pushed to define function and rationale by establishing campus purpose. A clear campus purpose, serving as a centering construct, can balance the tension between planned actions and change.

For any proposed initiative at UMR I could always ask myself, Does it promote student learning and development in the undergraduate health sciences that is distinctive, value added, and world class? I remember an encounter with an outstanding faculty member who was a core member of the team of faculty designing and implementing an integrated curriculum in the health sciences. The faculty member wanted to launch a major in her academic discipline. I said no because starting discipline-based majors was not aligned with campus purpose. I said no, knowing that the faculty member would probably leave UMR. We did lose her, but the faculty member understood the campus purpose and she understood the reason why I said no.

In other cases, community members pushed for new graduate-level programs that would address educational needs of the region. For example, local community members wanted graduate entrepreneurship programs, master programs in education, nursing, business, and social work. I said no because these academic programs were not aligned with campus purpose.

However, I discovered that I could say no and still be emphatic and supportive of the community's requests. The supplementary educational needs of the community could be met by partnering with other institutions. These institutions delivered their academic programs at UMR and addressed the educational needs of the region. UMR structured the educational partnerships in a cost-neutral fashion. I insisted that the partnering institutions were highlighted in any marketing materials to recruit students into the supplemental educational programs to avoid any confusion about the UMR campus purpose.

Some UMR Originators and other community members were critical of my decision to outsource these potential money-making graduate programs. And by now, you know that the ghost does not like outsourcing, especially educational programs. However, my experience was that the enrollments in these graduate programs were volatile and economy-driven, particularly in small to medium-size communities like Rochester. The programs did not generate a consistent revenue and needed to be subsidized during down periods. Even if the programs were cost-neutral or even profitable, they consumed organizational energy and mental attention that would distract from executing the campus purpose.

The middle years were also challenging for faculty and staff. They were overwhelmed by the daily minutia of operating the new campus. The ad hoc decision-making that is often associated with building a start-up was taking its toll on all of us. Tensions emerged, and faculty and staff were stressed.

When building something new, especially in a start-up mode, I simply could not anticipate how all the moving parts fit together.

I didn't build many "procedural" sidewalks because the paths everyone would follow to get the work done were unknown. Without sidewalks, we were all getting muddy.

It was during this time, which I now refer to as the stabilization planning stage, when we, as a purpose-driven campus, focused on building procedural sidewalks—the administrative processes, the operational procedures, hiring the right people with the right skill sets, and reorganizing ourselves to work more efficiently. We learned a lot from flying the plane and we now better understood the pressure points.

One product of the stabilization planning was the position prioritization process. There were many requests for new positions during the start-up mode. I listened to individual requests and often acknowledged to the person who made the request that a new position was probably needed. Later I frequently discovered that the financial resources were not available for the hire, which obviously frustrated the person making the request. The new position requests were presented individually and distributed throughout the fiscal year so there was no opportunity to compare or prioritize the requests. Some new position requests which seemed critical at one point became less critical later as we learned how to do our work differently. I wasn't managing physical and mental energies in making decisions about new positions and realized I needed to leverage the faculty and staff network.

We designed a position prioritization process that empowered the faculty and the staff in the different units to rank their requests for new positions. The leaders of the different units met and reviewed the requests from all units. They made joint recommendations to the senior leadership team. The senior leadership team reviewed the requests. The leadership team generated a list of positions to be filled, placed some on a prioritized waiting list depending on the overall funding for the next fiscal year, and designated which positions would not be funded nor considered further. We also included in the review replacements for positions when someone left the institution, with the caveat that the position may need to be filled immediately given the nature of the position.

The centralized process for prioritizing and filling new positions enabled the network of faculty and staff to direct strategic growth aligned with campus purpose. It created ways for faculty and staff who tended not to interact with each other about new positions to consider new and innovative ways to get the work done. It also provided a means to move resources around the organization that most benefited campus purpose rather than promote the growth of one unit.

Another example of stabilization planning was how we worked together to address enrollment volatility. During the start-up phase, we made many ad hoc (and probably ill-informed) decisions about how to recruit students. After we graduated several classes, we asked our graduates why they were attracted to UMR and why they were successful at UMR.

Our graduates told us that they attended UMR because they had a passion to care for and serve others. Our graduates came to UMR as first-year students with a fire already inside them that resulted from some life experience, often a traumatic one relating to their own health or that of a loved one. UMR nurtured their passion, but UMR did not instill in them their passion to care for or serve others. They told us they were attracted to a place where the campus and its community embodied their passion to serve and care for others in a health setting. They were less concerned about experiencing a traditional college campus life.

Finally, our graduates frequently demonstrated during their time as students that their passion made them resilient and enabled them to persevere in a rigorous program.

Based on these conversations with our graduates, we tailored our recruitment approach by engaging with students who expressed a passion to care for others and who demonstrated resilience through perseverance.

These traits were often exhibited by potential students who were of low socioeconomic means, first generation, or students of color. We learned from simultaneously building and flying the plane that these passionate and resilient underrepresented students also excelled in the purpose-driven structure. The success rates for underrepresented students were very similar to their peers.

We certainly hoped that the purposeful structure supported the success of all students, but we really didn't know. Today, UMR recognizes that making the campus more welcoming adds further value to the campus purpose by diversifying the health care workforce, makes UMR even more distinctive when the success rates of underrepresented students in the health sciences at UMR were compared with national rates, and makes UMR world class through its growing reputation to develop the potential of all students.[1]

We learned from flying the plane that the purpose-driven campus worked for passionate, resilient, and diverse students. We learned how to stabilize first-year enrollments. Faculty, staff, and students developed processes and procedures to better execute the purpose of the campus, and their capacity to adapt and reload during the delivery of the embryonic program in order to optimize the knowing and becoming experiences of the undergraduate students never ceased to amaze me. They clearly reinforced my belief in the power of networks.

The hard work by the faculty, staff, and students also reminds me of another adage: ideas are easy, and implementation is hard. Much of what I describe in this book is about forming ideas for starting a new campus. The start-up stage was the easy part.

The hard part happened during the stabilization stage. The faculty and staff executed new mind-sets, they instilled new habits, and they wrote the procedural details for the new policies. They enriched and empowered the easy ideas by their hard work. In retrospect, my role as a leader was less transactional and more transformative, empowering faculty and staff by freeing them from obsolete and dysfunctional structures.

It was critically important to free the faculty and staff from the shackles of old mind-sets, common practices, and ingrained habits—the ghost of university past. Any change effort will be difficult to launch nor sustainable unless you stop the haunting by the ghost. Stated differently, my version of the famous Peter

Drucker saying is, "The ghost will eat your strategy for breakfast."[2]

I discovered that the best way to stop the haunting is to perform a ritual to excise the ghost of university past. The ritual involved engaging the faculty and staff in difficult, complex, but rewarding discussions about grounding values and centering aspirations aligned with campus purpose. The ritual shaped their new mind-sets, their new habits of interactions to accommodate the new interdependencies, and their new expectations for their campus with purpose.

My experience was that a diminished version of this ritual occurs during strategic planning at established institutions. However, conversations about values during a strategic planning exercise tended to be brief and superficial, dominated by tactical, operational, and fiscal concerns.

I learned at UMR that when faculty and staff collectively engaged in conversations about institutional values and shared aspirations, they engaged in conversations that connected them with campus purpose.

This is not to say that discussions about tactics are unimportant. A campus cannot deliver on its purpose without funding and the right procedures, which I learned during the stabilization stage. All institutions need both conversations. The grounding values and the centering aspirations aligned with campus purpose provide the guideposts for tactics and fiscal investment. Otherwise, what you do and how you do it may not align with who you are or why the campus exists.

When marketing a strategic plan, we must not only promote its tactical portion, but also promote the grounding values and centering aspirations aligned with purpose. In this way, the products of the shared conversations about values and aspirations can also be widely shared, lived, codified, reviewed, and revised over time. The values are important and we need to continually remind each other about them. It keeps you connected to campus purpose.

When I retired in 2017, the UMR community compiled a list of grounding values. Equally important, they developed a shared definition for each value and dialogued whether their interactions manifested the grounding values.

UMR'S GROUNDING VALUES WERE
- Respect: we value habits of interaction that demonstrate the worth and dignity of each person;
- Human potential: we value every person's capacity to learn, develop, imagine, create, and contribute;
- Community: we value collective work and a culture of trust that promotes collaboration, problem-solving, and partnerships while creating belonging, accountability, and courageous action;
- Diversity and inclusiveness: we value the range of human differences and the active pursuit and involvement of varied perspectives; and
- Evidence-based decision-making: we value strategic collection and careful assessment of data to inform our choices in all matters, including student learning and development.

They also developed a list of centering aspirations aligned with campus purpose:

- Devote our expertise and energy to student learning and development, choosing habits that enable us to thrive as a healthy, high-integrity community characterized by our values.
- Generate transformative contributions to the renewal of higher education, providing a collaborative environment of inquiry that allows innovative thought-leadership in teaching and learning; educational research; public engagement; organizational efficiency; and community integration.
- Enhance the diversity of the health care workforce, through intentional inclusivity emanating from our core commitment to respectful human relationships and permeating our habits of interaction in recruitment, teaching and learning, and the ongoing life of our UMR community.
- Optimize the established arenas of distinctiveness, assessing results to provide ongoing evidence for decision-making and

mindfully aligning emerging innovations with these established strengths.

- Sustain UMR as an innovative, educational enterprise, through increased enrollment of passionate, resilient students commensurate with the goals established in our enrollment management plan as well as increased strategic generation of mission-driven resources.
- Contribute significantly to the continued development of the Rochester community, through intentional partnership and initiatives.

When reading their lists and definitions for grounding values and centering aspirations, I recognized an embodiment of the design principles. They were empowering each other to work across faculty, staff, students, and the community. They were leveraging the power of their network. They acknowledged the need to adapt by committing to the active collection of data and evidence to inform future decisions. And they fully embraced a holistic view of student learning and development—knowing and becoming. They also recognized that their work was bigger than just UMR— it was a calling to share what they have learned with the rest of higher education.

The UMR plane began flying higher and faster after the faculty and staff completed their work on the grounding values and centering aspirations, which provided the reinforcing structure to extend our wings.

7

What I Learned about
Students and Faculty

Although the campus purpose provided me a means to say no to requests for nonessential new programs or peripheral initiatives, the campus purpose also empowered me to find a means to say yes to students. Leaders in higher education are always invited to attend events to support local community organizations and charities. It is important for a leader to be present and engaged in the community. You need to "show up." However, attending and supporting the whole host of community and charity events can become time consuming and expensive. I said yes to the invitations when I could involve students.

For example, leaders on behalf of their campus are often asked to purchase a table at an event, which typically is a set of eight to ten tickets. You can invite guests to join you at the table designated for the campus. A table of ten may cost a thousand dollars. A chancellor could be invited to attend thirty such events over the course of a year. I often accepted an invitation, purchased a table, and filled the table with students.

Learning today is about knowing and becoming. Embedding students into the community through their attendance at these events were "becoming" experiences for them. They met and interacted with many community leaders. They listened to great presenters at events sponsored by the Chamber of Commerce, Rotary,

NAACP, Diversity Council, Salvation Army, Intercultural Mutual Assistance Association, Art Center, Civic Theatre, The Reading Center, economic development organizations, and others. Potential donors, faculty, or staff at times joined us at a table, but the students always enriched the evening.

Arts organizations requested financial support from the campus to co-sponsor a performance. I would consider a request when the value of the financial support was returned in the form free tickets for students. Because open seats often were available at a performance, the approach served as a win-win for campus purpose and for the arts organization.

It is also a common practice for a campus president or chancellor to invite donors, alumni, and other guests to their residence for a dinner. It creates an intimate atmosphere to engage your guests and connect them with the campus. Because UMR did not have alumni, an accumulation of donors, or intercollegiate sports programs, I invited students to the residence for dinner. My intent was to invite every first-year student in groups of six to eight to join me for a nice dinner. The dinners were well attended—the students simply were unable to resist free food. It was another "becoming" experience for them.

The student dinners were easy to do during the early years when the first-year classes were small. The dinners became more time consuming as class sizes grew larger. I hosted several student dinners at the residence during some weeks. However, without question it was the best investment of my time as a leader who was building a new campus with this purpose.

I learned much about the students during these dinners. I became especially attached to the first cohort of UMR students. I asked our first students why they came to UMR. Although they all wanted to pursue a health-related career, the other common theme was that they were excited about being part of something brand new. I began to refer to them as the "trailblazers." They were an adventurous group, never shy to put themselves out there to do things in the community. They started traditions that continue today, like a ballroom dance club that involved nearly half of their class, or a Halloween costume contest in which the entire class and many faculty and staff competed. In many ways, the trailblazers built student life at UMR.

Initially, there were concerns about what students would do for student life in the City for Health. The trailblazers taught us that student life at its core is about students hanging out together, being part of a social group that is supportive of each other. For many students at established institutions, roommates and other students in close proximity often attend different classes, at different schedules, and have different passions and interests. A student life needs to be constructed to create the common experiences that form the supporting relationships among students.

At UMR, the common experience was created by the curricular structure. Students were already hanging out together because of the teamwork design. The UMR students' lives were synchronized since their work products and tests were on the same schedule because of the cohort structure of the curriculum. Their fraternities or sororities were organic chemistry, sociology, philosophy, or Co-Lab. With this social structure already in place, they would build additional student life experiences by developing their own intramural volleyball league, going bowling at a local alley, cooking shared meals, attending UMR talent shows, starting a dance team or a chorale group, attending poet's night at a coffee shop, going swimming at the YMCA, or finding other ways to just "hang out together."

The trailblazers not only taught us about student life, they also provided an assessment of their learning experiences created by the evolving curricular model. In fact, the trailblazers referred to themselves as the "guinea pigs," because they knew the faculty and staff were "flying and building the plane at the same time." But the experimental nature of the curriculum didn't seem to bother them. They were a resilient and passionate group. They had as much to do with UMR's early success as any group.

I distinctly remember a curricular conversation with a trailblazer who came to the residence for dinner. One of my routine questions was to ask students what was their favorite class. Some students would identify a favorite course, but often students said that they could not decide between organic chemistry and philosophy. That response was very pleasing to the ears of someone wanting to build an integrated curriculum. One evening in response to my routine question, a trailblazer told me that he hated statistics. He could not wait for the statistics course to end.

Several years later this trailblazer returned to the residence to join a group of first-year students for dinner. In subsequent years, I often invited a junior or senior to join the dinner. The upper class students engaged with and answered the questions by the first-year students better than I did. After I asked my routine question about a favorite course, the now junior trailblazer interjected with his own story about how he answered my question two years earlier with, "I hate statistics!"

He told the first-year students that he was only exposed to statistics during his first semester. During his sophomore and junior years, he used statistics often in his courses and projects. He applied statistical concepts and tests to answer questions that he found interesting and important. He now much better understood and appreciated the value of statistics. He assured the first-year students that they will learn statistics over their four years at UMR.

Interestingly, this trailblazer who hated statistics as a first-year student completed a master's degree in international public health in England after graduation. At the time of this writing, he is working for a foundation and doing analyses of the health care infrastructure for a nation in Africa. He uses statistics in impactful ways every day.

I also asked students about their volunteer activities during the dinners. One student shared with me that she volunteered at a hospice facility. I asked her what she did at the hospice facility. She said that she was partnered with a client who she would visit several times each week. I asked what she did during her visits. She said it was really up to the client. If the client wanted to chat, they would talk. If the client wanted to play cards, they would play cards. I asked her if she worked with multiple clients. She said that she did, but only one client at a time. She would be with one client until the person passed, and then she would be partnered with a new client.

The routine nature of her response to my question surprised me. This seemed to be a lot to ask of a college student. I confessed to her that my tendency was to run from death and not embrace it. She told me that it was a privilege to be with a person at this time during their life journey, as it is a privilege to be present during a birth. What a "becoming" answer! The students taught me to "become" as well.

The other thing that students taught me about was resilience. In retrospect, I believe today that the faculty and staff at UMR survived its start-up and stabilization periods due in part to the inspiration provided by the resilience and persistence of the students. If the students can do this, so can we.

Many students at the dinners shared with me a story about how they, a parent or relative, or close friend dealt with a serious illness. These traumatic experiences put their own life in perspective and conditioned them to manage stress and challenges. Their world did not implode if they received a C on an organic chemistry test. It was clear to me during these dinner conversations that UMR students were pursuing health-related careers for all the right reasons.

Their persistence was also evident when I heard their stories about financial challenges. Many students worked part-time jobs during the week and on the weekends to cover their student expenses. They were very busy between working, too many hours in my estimation, and taking a full-time rigorous curriculum. The students needed to practice their time management skills daily.

A shy student told me at a dinner that she couldn't afford to live in student housing. She found a less expensive living arrangement, which sounded like a small hotel room that contained not much more than a bed and a shower. She lived alone, and understandably, she spent much of her time on campus. I saw her most mornings as I walked to my office studying alone in the student commons area. When I left at night, I often saw her studying at the same place. Greeting her in the morning and saying good-bye in the evening became part of my daily routine. She was always friendly. The only thing that I really knew about her was that she worked hard.

Several years later, I spent the night at the sleep clinic at the Mayo Clinic to determine if I had sleep apnea. To my surprise and absolute delight, when I woke up at the sleep clinic, I was greeted by this formerly shy student. I once again said "good morning" to her. She was now much more outgoing and confident. She was enrolled in respiratory care of the Bachelor of Science in Health Professions program. She was doing a rotation in the sleep clinic when I was being tested.

She graduated from UMR, received her certification, and now practices respiratory care. She visited me in my office after graduation prior to moving for her new position in respiratory care. We had a picture taken with us standing next to each other. When I now look at the picture, I immediately remember saying "good morning" and "good evening" to her as she studied in the student commons area.

The picture also reminds me about the privilege that I had as a chancellor to be part of our students' life journeys. As I tell all students at commencement, I can guarantee that if you don't work hard, you will not succeed. But I cannot guarantee that if you work hard, you will succeed. When you work hard and succeed, we need to celebrate. It is inspiring to witness their hard work, resilience, and perseverance, and we must celebrate their success. It is better than winning a conference championship game.

I could write many additional stories about student persistence to become a physician assistant, a chiropractor, a prosthetist, a child care specialist, an occupational therapist, a surgical assistant, a mental health counselor, a genetic counselor, a practitioner of naturopathic medicine, a sonographer, an environmental public health expert, a bioengineer, and yes, a medical doctor. Students are resilient when they have a passion.

However, sometimes passion finds the student with resilience. A student at UMR was having academic struggles. She worked very hard, but there were several courses that she just couldn't master. She tried several times without success. Because of her lack of success in these courses, no one could fault her if she decided to change her major, which meant leaving UMR. For some reason, she kept trying, and with the full support of her student success coach and the faculty, she finally mastered the content in those courses.

This was just her first hurdle. She applied to the Bachelor of Science in Health Professions program in one of the allied health fields. Her next punch was that she was not admitted. I spoke with the student after she received the rejection letter and asked why she applied to an allied health program that was diagnostic in nature. I thought she wanted to provide more direct health care. She told me that she hadn't thought about it in that way, so she reapplied to the bachelor's program, but this time in respiratory care. She was admitted.

She completed the respiratory care program, graduated, and received her certification to practice. She later told me that respiratory care was her life calling. It was a passion that found her. She showed me a picture of her standing in a blue uniform in front of a Mayo Clinic helicopter. One of her current responsibilities was to fly on the helicopter and manage the respiration of premature babies in transport to the Mayo Clinic. She is literally now flying with her passion.

It was a gift for me to spend time with the students at the dinners. For me, my conversations with the students reminded me and reinforced the campus purpose. At the dinners, the students expressed in their own words about how the faculty created in them a sense of belonging, a connection to each other, the campus, and the community. The students entrusted the faculty to shape their learning journey. Their trust was pervasive, not limited to a few faculty members or a few academic disciplines. My impression was that the students bestowed their broad trust in the faculty because they sensed that the faculty were uniformly and collectively committed to their learning and development.

Some of my colleagues, both custodial and change leaders, were concerned that I would not be able to hire faculty who were willing to set aside their disciplinary allegiance, work together with faculty from other disciplines, and deeply commit and conduct research on student learning and development. I did acknowledge that it would be difficult to hire faculty steeped in learning research. This is one of the reasons why I believed that a campus dedicated as an institution to conduct research on student learning and development added significant value. Some job applicants were simply seeking employment where they could continue a focus on their academic discipline without any real commitment to student learning, but their intent and priorities were obvious during the interviews.

However, many applicants for faculty positions exhibited a hidden passion to study and improve the ways students learn and develop in higher education, and they showed this deep commitment during the interview. Some came from established institutions and almost seemed relieved to express an interest in understanding student learning and development. They concealed their interest in student learning research at their previous department to not raise concerns among their faculty peers about their commitment to their discipline and disturb the ghost. The applicants who were recent PhD graduates tended to be less reserved and more open about their interest in conducting research on student learning. Both groups were competitive for positions at UMR.

My bet was that the tenure-track, learning-design faculty we hired could redirect their research prowess and training and apply it to study student learning and development. Some new UMR faculty were able to bridge this transition; others did not. The attrition rate for new tenure-track faculty at UMR, when calculated from the beginning of the probationary period to tenure, was around 50 percent. This attrition rate was similar to rates observed at other established institutions. You might be tempted to assume that it was easier for faculty from the social sciences and humanities to make the transition from their discipline-based scholarship to research student learning than for faculty from the physical, chemical, or biological sciences. However, thus far no disciplinary pattern was evident in the tenure decisions at UMR.

About half the faculty at UMR were student-based faculty. Based on my interactions with them during my time at UMR, I discovered that they fell into two general groups. One group felt that the position of a student-based faculty member was their life calling. They were energized by the constant interactions with students, sharing in their struggles and successes. They also enjoyed the interaction with their peers and sharing a common passion developing human potential.

The second group viewed the position of a student-based faculty as a residency, much like a medical residency, in which new doctors immerse themselves in health care to learn about the practice of medicine. This group of student-based faculty deeply immersed themselves in student learning to learn the practice of teaching and learning. They leveraged their experience working in a place focused on student learning and development to land new positions, some being tenure-track positions.

When I first noticed the relatively high turnover for the student-based faculty, I was concerned that the position and the work were unattractive or unrewarding. I heard the opposite in exit interviews. They accomplished their goal. They learned about student learning and were ready to practice teaching and learning in a different setting at a different institution. Although the students and I were always disappointed to see them leave UMR, I took solace in knowing that UMR, in some small way, promoted student learning and development in the twenty-first century through the spread of student-based faculty. When we hired replacements for faculty who departed, the new faculty brought with them new ways of thinking about student learning and development. The new blood kept us on our toes and forced us to be adaptive.

This academic structure, which targets the investment of faculty talents, their mental energies, and the power of a faculty network, was designed to implement the campus purpose. It is not the structure proffered by the ghost of university past, and the ghost did not make it easy to implement it. As I mentioned earlier in the book, ideas are easy and implementation is hard. It was relatively straightforward to develop ideas about ways to deploy faculty talents being mindful of the planning assumptions. The hard work was done by the learning-design and the student-based faculty in implementing these ideas within a faculty governance system that fully leveraged the network of talent across the institution shaped by a common passion to develop human potential. They overcame the ghost of university past and the cultural underpinnings associated with different academic disciplines and with tenure versus nontenure. The collective faculty truly did the hard work.

Many faculty care deeply about student learning and development. They express that passion in their research and in their teaching when they are freed from the ghost of the university past. What I have learned about faculty is consistent with the conclusions of Zemsky, Wegner, and Duffield, in *Making Sense of the College Curriculum* (2018), in which they share many faculty stories from across a variety of established higher education institutions about teaching and learning and pedagogical innovation. The authors conclude:

> We have learned much about how faculty view their worlds—and were often impressed by the intense commitment embedded in their calling as teachers. Most often, they had a passion that derived from the satisfaction found not just in contributing to but actually shaping the student's learning. What they sought as faculty members were learning environments that prepared their students for the many futures they envisioned. (163)
>
> What our story telling has taught us is simple enough to summarize. Curricular change is really tough for lots of reasons. Curricular change, unlike pedagogical innovation, requires collective action. A whole system has to change, often in its entirety. Everyone must adapt to the new rules. . . . (167)[1]

When empowered with new mind-sets, new rules of engagement, and new incentives, the UMR faculty by working collaboratively designed, implemented, and researched active learning experiences in a coordinated, integrated, community-immersed curriculum that is distinctive, world class, and value added to the students and the community.

Robert Zemsky has written about transformation in higher education for more than twenty years. In *Checklist for Change: Making American Higher Education a Sustainable Enterprise*, he argued that transformation has faltered in our business because all the change efforts have worked around the faculty, rather than being led by the faculty.[2] I agree. Sustainable institutional change requires that you leverage the network and tap into the passion of the faculty and staff to develop human potential.

8

Leading by Purpose in Higher Education

Robert Zemsky in his book *Checklist for Change: Making American Higher Education a Sustainable Enterprise* refers to UMR as a micro-model and a vehicle for change. He states in the book that I kept it simple.[1]

When I chat with my colleagues about UMR, they also remark that I kept it simple. They attribute what we accomplished at UMR to keeping it simple. The campus is small, compact, focused, and not capital intense. However, they also believe that what we learned at UMR would not apply to them since their campuses are large, complex, and capital intense. UMR kept it simple, but their campuses were more complicated.

As I reflect back, my experience at UMR certainly didn't feel simple. I shared stories in the previous chapters about the many complexities that I managed starting a campus from scratch. I believe what my colleagues meant when saying that UMR was simple was it had a singular campus rationale and function (purpose). My leadership colleagues at established institutions were managing multiple purposes, which made their leadership challenges more complex.

Whether or not the wide range of functions of established campuses was by design or the product of spurious expansion over the decades, the reality is that higher education leaders today are managing multiple campus purposes. This is why my leadership colleagues tend to dismiss any lessons that emerged from building a campus with a purpose because it will not generalize to a campus with many purposes.

As I mentioned in the preface, the reason for writing this book was that starting a new campus was a unique leadership experience and created an extraordinary opportunity for me to view higher education through a different lens. This new perspective made me think about why the campus exists. The lesson that I learned and want to share with my colleagues is that there is great value in leading by purpose, even if you have multiple purposes.

A prevailing habit in higher education was to blend all purposes together without prioritization in a mission statement, in the organizational structures, and in the funding algorithms. One must first disentangle the different purposes and consider the rationale for each in order to begin to understand how a campus fulfills and prioritizes each purpose. For many established institutions, there were specific rationales for the purposes of undergraduate education, graduate/professional education, research, continuing education and extension, hospitals, and intercollegiate athletics. The scope of the operation associated with each purpose varies by the type of institution. Some institutions have small or no graduate/professional programs. Some institutions are research intensive. Some have land grant missions with extension programs. And some will have hospitals.

Once the primary campus purposes are identified, the next step is to ask two questions: How does the campus manage a distinct purpose across different organizational units? How does the campus manage across different purposes?

A way to begin to answer the question about purpose and organizational structure is to review the campus's organizational chart. Established campuses typically have organizational units associated with undergraduate education, graduate/professional education, research, colleges and academic departments, intercollegiate athletics, hospitals, continuing education or extension, finance and operations, fund-raising and alumni activities, and a sundry of other smaller organizational units.

The different organizational units can be grouped by each purpose, knowing that there will be some clustering and overlap between different organizational units and a campus purpose. The finance and operation cluster (e.g., finance and budgeting, facilities management, human resources, information technology, general counsel, marketing and university relations, governmental relations, and so forth) and the fund-raising unit can be removed from this analysis. These are enabler units and not purpose driven. These organizational units enable a campus to deliver on its purposes. The exception is that for-profit institutions have a purpose to make money.

For the campus purpose of undergraduate education, there is overlap between the organizational unit responsible for undergraduate education and the colleges and academic departments. Both play roles in the delivery of undergraduate instruction. As one continues the analysis for campus purposes of graduate/professional education, research, and continuing education and extension, one discovers that the colleges and academic departments are central players to the execution of at least four of the purposes of a campus. Given the central role played by the different colleges and their academic departments in executing multiple purposes, it is not surprising that college deans are major decision makers and yield significant influence at many established campuses.

The common practice in higher education is to embed the administrative function associated with a campus purpose into the overall operation of the colleges and their academic departments. The organizational structure is built around an academic discipline and not a campus purpose.

An organizational structure built around academic discipline makes it difficult to directly manage and prioritize different campus purposes. A disciplined-based organizational structure distributes the responsibility to execute a campus purpose. The structure also enables the different colleges or academic departments to manage different campus purposes with differing priorities.

A distributed, discipline-based organizational approach to manage different campus purposes may be appropriate if all the colleges and academic departments have similar viewpoints, priorities, and centering aspirations for each purpose. However, my experience is that deans operate their colleges differently. Their rationale is that undergraduate education, graduate/professional education, research and scholarship, and continuing education vary by academic discipline; hence, the different campus purposes must be managed within the unique context of an academic discipline.

The deans' argument would surely seem to apply for the management of the campus purposes of research and scholarship, and many discipline-specific, research-based graduate/professional programs. Nonetheless, there is a trend in many research fields and areas of scholarship in which the topics are crossing disciplinary boundaries. As a consequence, some argue that graduate and professional students should develop more interdisciplinary skills.

The deans' disciplinary argument is less applicable for undergraduate education. An integrated and interdisciplinary approach creates an undergraduate learning environment that better empowers students to know and become and be prepared for exponential times.

The lesson that I learned at UMR is that there are merits to exploring a non-discipline-based, centralized structure focused on executing a single campus purpose. It is a very different organizational model, and one that can only be explored if a campus is willing to free itself from the ghost of the university past.

The prevailing practice is to hire faculty primarily for their content expertise in their academic discipline. They reside in the different colleges and academic departments and work independently to deliver individual general education courses. In contrast, imagine a non-disciplined-based, centralized structure that administratively houses a faculty charged to develop foundational knowledge and skills in a common curriculum. This new structure assembles a faculty and staff who have backgrounds in learning research and student development, who are singularly focused on undergraduate education, and work collaboratively to build a common learning experience for undergraduates. The new faculty and staff would not only expose students to different ways of knowing through the lens of different academic disciplines, but also design intentional experiences across courses in the curriculum so students become critical thinkers, interculturally competent, team players, and so on.

An intentional development of the "becoming" skills in undergraduates is very difficult to implement in a disciplined-based, distributed organizational structure involving all the colleges and academic departments.[2] In my opinion, and based on what I observed at UMR, the best way to achieve the distinct campus purpose of undergraduate education is to assemble a faculty in a new undergraduate education unit whose sole purpose is to design and deliver the learning experiences to develop the foundation skills of the students. The "undergraduate faculty" are evaluated for tenure or promotion in accordance with guidelines aligned with delivering the campus purpose of undergraduate instruction. The undergraduate faculty, who possess varied expertise covering different academic disciplines, deliver the first two years of the curriculum, designing common learning experiences that empower students to know and become and prepare them for exponential times.

The undergraduate students select a major field a study for their last two years of the curriculum. The faculty in the colleges and the academic departments design and shape their curricula to build on the foundation knowledge and skills and develop the specific knowledge and skills required in a particular academic field. Having faculty in academic departments focus on upper division, discipline-specific courses better aligns with their content expertise and disciplinary interest. It also enables them to channel their mental energy on graduate education and research and scholarship.

Some will criticize any approach that organizationally separates the faculty responsible for foundation learning and the faculty responsible for learning in an academic field. The critics will say there is not enough room in the 120 credit hour undergraduate curriculum to support both a common foundation of learning and a major. A credit hour analysis, however, reveals there is ample credit hour space in a baccalaureate degree program to do both. A typical major requires around 40 credit hours, and most general education requirements are also around 40 credit hours. The remaining 40 or so credit hours could be distributed differently; some diverted into intentional foundation learning, and some used by students to take prerequisite courses for specific majors (e.g., the higher-level math courses required for engineering majors).

Today, these open, nonprescribed 30–40 credit hours are taken as elective courses. Students do use this curricular space to explore new topics and interests. However, many students also use this opening in the four-year curriculum to take different prerequisite courses because they switched their majors.

There is value to students taking elective courses, but is their value justified by the high tuition costs? It has been suggested that by removing the elective portion of a curriculum the cost of undergraduate degree could be lowered by shortening the degree to 90 credit hours, making a baccalaureate a three-year degree.[3] I lean toward needing all four years to prepare students to know and become for exponential times. However, we must be more prescriptive and intentional in designing the learning experiences for students across all four years.

Some deans and department chairs will worry that the approach of breaking undergraduate instruction into two distinct parts, foundation and major field, and having their faculty no longer teaching general education courses, will financially hurt their colleges and their academic units. The current internal funding models at most established institutions are enrollment driven. It follows that the colleges or academic departments will lose funding when their faculty are no longer offering enrollment-rich general education courses. However, these funding concerns are remediated simply by changing the internal budgeting algorithm.

I learned at UMR that there are significant advantages to a foundation learning approach. It focuses on developing foundation knowledge and skills in students; it is less expensive to implement because fewer courses need to be offered than in a traditional general education model; and it allows more time for students to discover their nexus between passion and ability.

However, the custom of higher education is to blend, distribute, separate by academic discipline, and delegate the responsibility to deliver on many campus purposes to the colleges and academic departments. This might not always be the best approach. Any overall strategy to deliver on any one campus purpose is weakened by the dynamics of managing the various mind-sets, aspirations, and cultures of the different colleges and academic departments. The leader directs resources and mental energy managing colleges and academic departments rather than directly investing those resources and mental energy on campus purposes.

I learned at UMR that a centralized focus on a campus purpose is a more effective and efficient way to deliver a purpose. If we can free our thinking from the grasp of the ghost of the university past and examine purposes separately, a leader of a campus can explore new and better ways to empower and align the strengths of the faculty and staff to deliver each purpose.

To further add to the complexity of a campus with multiple purposes, not only does a leader manage a multifaceted organizational structure to deliver on each purpose, but the leader must also manage across all purposes. How does a leader manage across distinct functions in order to optimize fulfilling all campus purposes? Are there trade-offs due to limited resources? How does a leader prioritize one purpose over another?

There are trade-offs related to limited financial resources. However, there are also trade-offs related to limited time and mental energy. Leaders can be dominated by the challenges related to one campus purpose, for whatever reason, and consequently they do not devote the appropriate attention to other critical campus purposes.

I can remember chatting with a president about the learning innovations at UMR. The president responded, half-jokingly but sadly, "What is student learning?" The president regretted that he could not find the time to be more directly connected with undergraduate learning at his institution. I noticed over the past ten years that my conversations with my leadership colleagues were prolonged and studied if we were talking about fund-raising, research productivity, or intercollegiate athletics. My conversations with them about student learning and development were more one-sided and short. This sounds like a criticism of my colleagues, but it is their reality because of the complexity of managing multiple campus purposes. There are times when an issue with a campus purpose will gobble up, often involuntarily, all the mental energy of a leader. Just ask any college president who is, for example, dealing with an athletic scandal. Many higher education leaders will commiserate with each other that they often feel that they are "chasing and not leading."

One way leaders manage and prioritize, either knowingly or unwittingly, multiple purposes is through cross-subsidization.[4] Cross-subsidization is a budgeting process in which surplus resources generated by one entity are used to support the activities of another entity. Consider the differential cost of instruction for different academic disciplines.[5] It is important that a campus offers both physics and sociology classes. Both courses are needed to fulfill the purpose of undergraduate education. However, the cost of instruction for a physics course is higher than for sociology. The tuition generated by the students taking a sociology course is greater than its cost of instruction (surplus). The tuition generated by students taking a physics course is less than the cost of instruction (deficit). The surplus of revenue generated by the students taking the sociology course is used to cover the deficit incurred by offering the physics course.

Cross-subsidization is typically not managed on a course-to-course basis. The overall cost of instruction for all courses, even though some courses generate a surplus and some incur a deficit, is covered by a pool of funds generated by student tuition, or at a public institution, plus state allocations. Given the current mix of student tuition and state support, student tuition is the primary revenue source for most institutions. The cross-subsidization process is invisible to most. Considering the aforementioned example, some sociology department chairs may be aware that they are not receiving their total allocation of student tuition.

Clearly a leader does not subsidize an operation with a distinct purpose if that entity generates sufficient revenue to cover its expenses. Fund-raising and alumni support is an example of an entity that generates not only resources to support its activities but also generates funds to support other functions of the different campus purposes. That is its enabling purpose. Having stated this, there are often discussions about how much of the revenue generated by a fund-raising organization should be used to cover its expenses and how much should be allocated to support other campus purposes. It is a healthy discussion about optimizing a return on the investment by alumni and donors.

There are other organizational units for which a subsidy is needed to supplement the revenue to cover the overall expenses. Some of the units requiring a subsidy address different campus purposes. The cross-subsidization nature of the budgeting process must be strategic when the pooled revenues are used to subsidize different campus purposes. Should undergraduate tuition or allocations from the state support graduate and research programs or intercollegiate athletics? Does the amount of cross-subsidization reflect any priorities for the different campus purposes?

Most graduate programs tend to cost more than the revenue generated by graduate tuition. The exception may be the graduate programs that are considered more professional-based, such as the MBA, MPA, or masters programs in education. Graduate courses by their very nature have very small enrollments and are generally taught by faculty with the highest salaries. In some cases, graduate students do not directly pay tuition. Their tuition costs are covered as part of their teaching assistantships or by research grants. Nevertheless, generally the resources generated by the higher graduate tuition, research grants, and the replacement costs related to their teaching assistantships do not offset the full cost of research-based graduate programs. Hence, many graduate programs are subsidized by revenue generated by undergraduate student tuition and from state allocations for public institutions.

Does this cross-subsidy reflect the campus's prioritization for graduate instruction over undergraduate education? The answer may be yes. Does the cross-subsidy unwittingly dilute the purposes of both undergraduate and graduate education? These important strategic questions are raised by the cross-subsidization for different campus purposes.

The cross-subsidization of the research function is another important strategic question that needs to be addressed by a campus leader. Many believe that research grants cover the cost of doing research. I have not met a single research administrator who concurs. Many research administrators are involved in intense discussions with the federal research organizations about indirect cost recovery. They negotiate with agency representatives to secure funds to cover the full cost of doing research on their campuses. Indirect cost recovery, sometimes referred to as F&A (facilities and administrative) costs, are the extra costs incurred by doing research not covered by the grant. Research grants only partially cover the costs associated with the use and maintenance of campus facilities where the research is conducted and with the additional costs incurred by a research administration that provides regulatory oversight necessary to conduct the research. The deficit problem related to research is exacerbated by researchers and campuses who waive the current indirect costs paid by the federal research organizations in order for the researcher to receive a larger grant to conduct research—more for the research, less for the campus to cover its full costs.

The federal research agencies take the position that the campus should share in the cost of research. If they fully covered all the indirect costs incurred by a campus, there would be less funds to support the actual research. Non-federal sources of research funding, such as state programs or research grants provided by the private sector, also want to direct most, if not all, of their investment into the research. This is their justification for why they will either not reimburse or will under-reimburse a campus for any indirect costs associated with conducting the research.

It follows that the more research grants awarded to a campus, regardless of the source, the greater the subsidy required by the campus to cover the full costs associated with the campus purpose of research. Depending on the size of the campus research program, the unreimbursed indirect research costs can be tens of millions of dollars.

When I was in Missouri, there was an effort to increase overall research funding, particularly for the large comprehensive campus. An analysis was shared with me that showed a significant correlation between the amount of federal research funding and the resources generated by the tuition and the level of state funding. The institutions with more state funding and more tuition revenue generated by a larger undergraduate enrollment tended to secure more federal research dollars. The conclusion drawn from the analysis was that without significant state support and the tuition revenue generated by a large undergraduate enrollment, a campus does not have the resources to cross-subsidize all the costs of doing research and support the graduate students who assist in doing the research. A limited capacity to cross-subsidize restricted the research capacity of the campus.

The cross-subsidization of research is invisible to many on campus because of the pooling of tuition and state funds in the budgeting process. Another less visible way a campus cross-subsidizes the research purpose is through its allocation of faculty time and effort. A prevailing habit for many established institutions is to allocate faculty effort according to a 40–40–20 formula: 40 percent of faculty time is devoted to instruction; 40 percent to research and scholarship; and 20 percent to service. In some cases, a research grant covers a portion of the faculty's salary, but often a faculty member is released from teaching undergraduates to give them more time to do the research funded by the grant.

Like the blending of different campus purposes across the colleges and academic departments mentioned earlier, this is a similar blending of campus purpose, but across all faculty time and effort. Because a campus pays the full salary of a faculty member, in essence the campus has devoted 40 percent of its critical workforce to research and scholarship.

This distribution of faculty effort may align with a desired prioritization for the campus purposes of undergraduate instruction and research and scholarship. However, a campus instead could allocate 60 percent of the time of its faculty workforce to undergraduate instruction, and only 20 percent to research and scholarship and 20 percent to service. The campus could also allocate different distributions of effort for different faculty. Some faculty could devote 100 percent of their time to undergraduate instruction, and other faculty spend 100 percent of their time on research. If a campus freed itself from the ghost, it could examine if a different allocation of faculty effort or a differential approach to assigning faculty effort better aligns with a strategic prioritization for the campus purposes of undergraduate education and research and scholarship.

It is not my intent to recommend a distribution of faculty effort for different campus purposes. Different campuses have different priorities for different campus purposes. However, any allocation of faculty time across different campus purposes is a form of cross-subsidization, because undergraduate tuition and state support for public institutions are the primary sources of revenue covering the cost of faculty salaries. Because faculty salaries are a major cost driver for campuses, 40 percent of that overall cost must be considered a significant investment in research and scholarship.

Intercollegiate athletics creates another interesting strategic analysis related to the cross-subsidization of different campus purposes. Some challenge the notion that intercollegiate athletics has a distinct campus purpose. They say that the only campus purposes are teaching, research, and community engagement and service—the so-called tripartite mission of the university. Intercollegiate athletics is not core to the institution—participants in intercollegiate sports are students first and athletes second.

My argument is that today campuses involved in intercollegiate athletics, whether intended or not, are managing the campus purpose of entertainment. Intercollegiate sports are not just for the participating students. The rationale and function for intercollegiate athletics today is to entertain the general public.

Over my career, I have heard presentations about the non-entertainment aspects of intercollegiate sports. Athletic directors and coaches often talk about how participation in intercollegiate sports develops leadership, resilience, teamwork skills, and time management skills in their athletes. These are certainly important "becoming" traits to develop in our students, but we should develop leadership, resilience, teamwork, and time management skills in all our students, not just those with athletic abilities.

The marketing arm of a campus often refers to intercollegiate athletics as the "front porch of the campus." They make the case that the sports programs engage and connect the general public with the campus. Some also point out that enrollments are higher when the major intercollegiate sports programs perform well.

It follows that the rationale and defined purpose of intercollegiate athletics is to promote campus brand through sports entertainment. This places intercollegiate athletics in the category of the organizational units that are enablers, like the cluster of units related to finance and operation or fund-raising. These units enable and support the different campus purposes.

The effectiveness of the enabler units is evaluated by examining the return on investment. The amount of investment in fundraising is evaluated in the context on the amount raised versus cost of operation. The amounts invested in the different administrative operations—such as financial planning, budgeting, human resources, information technology, marketing, facilities management, and other administrative services—are evaluated in the context of cost versus the quality of services provided to achieve multiple purposes.

In the same way, the investment in campus branding via the intercollegiate sports programs should be evaluated in the context of achieving the multiple campus purposes. At UMR, I did not anticipate any significant return on an investment in intercollegiate athletics on the campus purpose of undergraduate health education and research on student learning and development. Hence, there was never any serious consideration of starting intercollegiate athletic programs at UMR.

However, the strategic question for established institutions is what is the return on its investment in sports entertainment on campus branding? The cost of the investment in intercollegiate athletics varies widely across campuses. The cost depends on the number of intercollegiate programs, the facilities, the conference, travel, athletic scholarships, event management, liability, and the salaries for coaches, trainers, and athletic administrators. The revenue generated by intercollegiate athletics also varies widely across campuses depending on stadium size, ticket sales, TV revenues, and fund-raising efforts. There have been a number of analyses over the years about the cross-subsidization of intercollegiate sports.[6] Although the revenue sources take many forms and amounts, it is clear that few, if any, intercollegiate sports programs have total revenues that exceed full costs. There is a financial cost to the campus to brand itself through sports entertainment. What is the return on the investment?

The major way intercollegiate sports programs positively impact campus brand is through winning. The pressure to win over the past several decades has driven up investment costs in intercollegiate athletics: higher coaching salaries, better athletic facilities, better training facilities, and better support and housing facilities for student athletes (athlete villages). The higher costs have driven up ticket prices, which makes it difficult for some students to attend sports events. Maybe this is why some campuses have levied an athletic student fee, whether or not the students attend sports events.[7]

The higher winning costs over the past several decades have increased the demand on campus fund-raising units to solicit support from donors and alumni to support athletic programs. Unfortunately, this dilutes the fund-raising efforts to support campus purposes by introducing a conflict for donors and alumni to support intercollegiate athletics versus the campus purposes of undergraduate education, graduate/professional education, and research and scholarship.

The costs to remain or become competitive in intercollegiate sports and positively impact the campus brand have clearly accelerated in recent times. However, there is another form of cost associated with intercollegiate athletics that is not financial but is directly related to campus brand and reputation. In the sports entertainment business, success is measured by how well you engage and connect a large community with the sports team. Successful intercollegiate sports programs also garner the attention of the sports media because their readership and viewership follow the sports teams. The intensity of the media interest in intercollegiate athletics makes me wonder who is promoting whose brand. Is the intercollegiate sports program promoting the campus brand, or is the campus brand promoting an intercollegiate sports program?

The challenge posed by this hyperattentive media environment is that a leader can lose control over campus brand and reputation. Improper and poor behaviors exhibited by coaches, athletic staff, and athletes, who have little knowledge of or commitment to multiple campus purposes, will negatively impact campus brand and reputation.

The campus brand and reputation is a critical asset. Protecting the overall reputation of a campus is one of the reasons why college presidents become directly involved in matters such as coach hiring, firing, setting salaries, athlete discipline, and other challenges associated with running an intercollegiate sports program. The irony is that the purpose of the intercollegiate sports program is to promote the campus brand, but often intercollegiate sports can be the source of negative media coverage. A college president can still lose on brand even if the sports team wins. All of this is just part of being in the sports entertainment business.

The reputational risks associated with negative media coverage of an intercollegiate sports program are real and distract campus leadership from other campus purposes. The other emerging risk to campuses with intercollegiate sports programs is a future liability related to injury and abuse. Actuaries have advised campuses in the past that it is more cost effective to cover liability risks with internal funds rather than incur the high cost of liability insurance. Consequently, most campuses are self-insured.

Today, the athletes participating in intercollegiate sports are larger, stronger, and faster. As a result, physical injuries are becoming more pervasive and serious in many of the contact sports. Unlike torn ligaments or broken bones, the most troubling aspect of the concussion injuries associated with contact sports is the delayed and permanent impact of the injury on cognitive functioning and mental health. Future liability costs associated with these injuries could be catastrophic for a campus and were probably not factored in prior actuarial recommendations for campuses to be self-insured.

The emerging liability risk associated with intercollegiate sports parallels similar concerns about managing the risks associated with operating a health care facility. Many campuses have historically operated a hospital to support medical training. Over the past several decades, health care has become more complex and litigious. To be competitive in today's volatile health care market requires taking more financial risks. Many campuses have found themselves deeply entrenched in operating not just a hospital, but an entire health care system in order to continue to provide clinical training for its students.

Some leaders have asked if a campus needs to be in both the health care and education business in order to provide clinical training and medical education. Some leaders decided to insulate the other campus purposes from the volatility of the health care market by developing a relationship with a separate legal entity to operate the hospital or the health care system. The legal entities take different forms: some campuses sold their hospital assets to a third party with the agreement to provide access for medical and clinical training for students; some campuses continue to own the hospital but have partnered with a separate entity to deliver the health care. These arrangements legally separate the responsibility for the hospital and health system operation from campus operation. In doing so, the campus insulated the purposes of undergraduate education, graduate/professional education, and research from the liability risks associated with being in today's health care marketplace.

In a similar way, as intercollegiate sports become more competitive and more money is involved in operating a sports entertainment business, the increasing risks and volatility associated with an intercollegiate sports program may push campus leaders to consider legal entities similar to those put in place to dampen the risks and volatility associated with operating hospitals and health care systems. Some campus leaders may decide that they do not need to be in both the sports entertainment business and the education business.

One could imagine in the near future campus leaders seeking a legal relationship with a new partner or with an existing entity that assumes the full responsibility and liability for operating the sports programs on campus. The sports entity would recoup all revenues but it also would cover its full costs, including liabilities related to sports injuries and other abusive behaviors.

The sports entity would rent and operate the sports venues on campus. The current discussion about the interplay between the student and the athlete parts of the student–athlete persona would be resolved by this approach. The athletes would be employees and paid in accordance with the revenues and policies of the sports entity. The athletes could attend the campus as a student at their discretion through a separate agreement with the campus. The athlete, now a student, would have the resources to pay the tuition costs and attend college at a time either during their athletic career or after, whenever the now student has the time and energy to devote to and be successful in knowing and becoming.

The campus would negotiate naming rights with the new sports entity. The campuses would have the leverage in these negotiations since they own the sports venues. The athletic conferences would still be comprised of the participating campuses, and collectively the campus presidents would regulate the overall operation of the intercollegiate athletic conference. The sports entertainment product would appear in many ways the same to the fans, just as it does for the patients served by a health care system with a university name but operating under a separate legal agreement.

This new organizational structure for intercollegiate athletics better aligns with being in the sports entertainment business. With this structure, a campus better manages the amount of or discontinues altogether any cross-subsidization from tuition and state funds to support intercollegiate athletics. The presidents retain more control on the branding and reputation of their campuses. They will no longer be held responsible for the hiring and firing of coaches, for high salaries of coaches, or for poor behavior by athletes and athletic staff. The fund-raising arm of the campus will no longer be conflicted between raising funds for the campus purposes and for intercollegiate athletics.

Some of my colleagues will frown on this recommendation to consider a separate entity to operate their sports programs. They will be concerned that their sports programs do not have a large following, the sports facilities are in the need of significant repair, and other marketing issues that would make their campus unattractive as a partner for a sports entity. I understand that this will probably be the case for many campuses in smaller athletic markets. My response would be to ask several questions. What is the purpose of your intercollegiate sports programs? Is the amount of subsidy from tuition and state resources allocated to the sports programs aligned with campus priorities for different campus purposes? How are you managing the liability risk associated with your sports programs? The answers to these strategic questions may provide the reasons for a campus leader to scale back or discontinue intercollegiate sports programs on their campus. More campus leaders are fighting the ghost of university past and making this hard decision.

The ghost of university past will respond vehemently even to the suggestion of re-examining the relationship of intercollegiate sports with the other campus purposes. Many campuses have been very successful in the sports entertainment business and over time have intertwined the constructs of sports and higher education. I battled the ghost in Rochester when I informed the community that I was not going to start intercollegiate sports programs. As I said earlier in the book, there are still some in the Rochester community who are disappointed that I did not build a "real" university. In their minds, a real university has intercollegiate sports.

In this chapter, I outlined what it means to lead by purpose in higher education. A purpose-driven analysis creates new ways, different from those of the ghost of university past, to think about graduate education, research, intercollegiate sports, and their relationship to undergraduate education. A purpose-driven analysis unravels the complexities of higher education, which is the first step for a campus community to answer strategic questions about how it manages and how it invests in multiple campus purposes.

9
Closing Comments

My reason for writing this book is not to promote one campus purpose over another. My reason is not to recommend fewer or more campus purposes. The discussion about undergraduate education, graduate/professional education, research, and intercollegiate athletics in the previous chapter was intended to be illustrative and thought provoking. How many campus purposes? How is each campus purpose managed? How is each funded and does the funding reflect intentional priorities? These are the critical strategic questions to be answered when leading by purpose.

The custom in higher education is to fuse multiple purposes together. We fuse together the resources in the budgeting process that funds them. We fuse together the responsibility to execute them in the colleges and academic departments. We fuse them together in faculty workload.

All the institutional mass action and inertia that results when the campus purposes are melded together will weaken the impact of any change. Maybe this is why my colleagues who I referred to as change leaders said that there are significant transaction costs associated with change. They had to overcome the power structures that emerged as a by-product of an institutional focus on academic discipline and the intermingling of campus purposes and funding. This structural dynamic of higher education stifles agility and the capacity for a campus to adapt during exponential times.

In building a campus from scratch, I was forced to think about why the campus exists? What is its purpose? How can a campus adapt to the ever-changing landscape of higher education and remain true to its purpose?

If you divorce the ghost of the university past, it becomes plausible to answer these strategic questions, not only for a new campus with a singular purpose, but also for a campus with multiple purposes. Once a leader disentangles the multiple purposes buried in its organizational structures and funding models, a leader can ask, How many purposes can I afford? Which ones are more important? How do I manage them? How do I fund each? The lesson that I learned and want to share is that there is great value in understanding and leading by purpose, even if you have multiple purposes.

When you are free from the shackles of the ghost of the university past, a leader can deploy new habits and new mind-sets. A leader can broach a discussion about the prioritization of multiple campus purposes. A leader can now lead a campus in discussions about rethinking undergraduate education and committing more institutional energy and resources on student learning and development. A leader can now unscramble the funding in the budgeting process derived from state and tuition revenues that fund and subsidize different campus purposes. A leader can now reexamine investments in real estate and building operation and the subsidies and liabilities associated with being in the sports entertainment business. A leader can now work with faculty and staff to reimagine grounding values and centering aspirations. This should be the overall framework for strategic planning on a campus.

Strategic planning discussions that focus on separate campus purposes will be intense and complex, but they will be substantive. The discussions will surface the core question. What is the campus purpose in the twenty-first century? These are the right conversations for leaders, for faculty, for staff, for students, and for stakeholders.

The conversations were complex and intense even when leading a campus with a singular campus purpose. Because we kept it simple at UMR, these conversations were manageable. I did not have to combat the inertia of discipline-based power structures. UMR, being new and compact, was strategically more maneuverable than larger and more complex established campuses.

I have used a metaphor about navigating the seas to describe the strategic role played by UMR. Many leaders in higher education feel as though they are steering large ships. These ships have much mass and inertia (e.g., multiple and fused purposes). The ships take a long time to turn. If the wind blows in the wrong direction (e.g., an athletic scandal), the ships may travel in an unintended direction.

It is understandable why many leaders are frozen at the helm. The seas are choppy. It is foggy. Knowledge generation and dissemination are changing. Learning is changing. Students are changing. Revenue sources are changing. These are exponential times. It is not clear where to steer the ship. They might not be able to correct course in time if they steer a ship in the wrong direction.

Along comes UMR. It is your scouting boat. It is simple and maneuverable. It can meander in the fog. If it approaches rocks, it can steer away before its crashes. And its leader can signal to the larger ships to steer away. In its travels, the scouting boat might find clear skies and smooth water. Its leader can signal to the other ships to steer in this direction.

I do not want to convey by the ship metaphor that I think UMR has done it better than other institutions, nor am I saying that other institutions should do it in the same way as I described in the book. UMR is probably already doing some things differently. I hope so. The adaptable institution will be ever changing and striving to do the right thing in the right way to survive in exponential times.

Along its journey UMR must embrace its role as a scouting boat and share what it has learned. The president of the university launched UMR over a decade ago to be a vehicle for change. This is encoded in its DNA.

I learned much over the last decade building a campus focused on developing human potential and being freed from the ghost of university past. I hope that you learned something from my story about building a campus with purpose. More important, I hope you have the chance to learn from UMR faculty, staff, community stakeholders, and the students—they are doing the hard part and writing the UMR story.

Epilogue

Purpose and Innovation

As I received feedback on earlier drafts of the book, I was struck by two implicit assumptions made by my colleagues about new campuses. The first assumption is that being new also means being innovative. The second assumption is that innovation is the driving force reshaping higher education.

A new campus is likely to be viewed as innovative because its new buildings have a modern design and are equipped with state-of-the-art technologies and audiovisual equipment. These fused precepts of new and innovative follow from a proposition made in the beginning of chapter 5. Many tend to associate a campus with its physical infrastructure and not with its people. It is the people who make a campus innovative.

Regarding the second assumption, I suspect that market dynamics and not innovation per se is also contributing to change in higher education. New institutions and new business models are created to fill new and changing markets. This raises some interesting scholarly questions about the interplay between market and innovation forces in the reshaping of higher education.

On the market side, do market dynamics drive the structure and culture of a new institution? Is the rationale to provide geographical access in open markets to simply extend familiar, standardized methods and processes (a franchise model)?

On the innovation side, does the nature of being embryonic embolden a new institution to explore and adopt more nonstandard, innovative approaches? Do the small size and simplicity of mission enable an institution to be structurally maneuverable and innovative?[1]

As I explained in this book, the primary rationale for the creation of UMR was not to address unmet educational needs in Rochester, Minnesota. The basic educational needs of the community were being addressed by other higher education institutions and by the delivery of off-site programming offered by the Twin Cities and Duluth campuses of the University of Minnesota. Also early in its genesis, many justified starting of a new campus in Rochester because it would create new markets by deploying new and innovative learning technologies.

In the end, UMR was shaped neither by a new market nor innovation. It was entirely built around a campus purpose—an undergraduate health campus researching student learning and development. Although innovation was not the driver, UMR was committed to explore innovation as a better means to deliver and sustain its purpose. UMR expanded the structural and process toolbox to ensure that it had access to the proper tools to build a purposeful campus. At times, standard and traditional tools were used (e.g., grades, course credits, tenure, among others). Other times, new and innovative tools were designed and deployed (e.g., no academic departments, a foundational and adaptable curriculum, a single degree platform, private-public partnerships, and so forth). UMR selected a structure, method, or approach, whether it was standard and traditional or new and innovative, that best executed the campus purpose.

The message embedded in the story of building UMR from scratch is that the reshaping of higher education must be driven by campus purpose. The landscape of higher education should not be reshaped only by innovation or only by markets. Innovation should support the campus purpose, and many open markets can be addressed by intercampus cooperation supported by new technologies. However, in parallel, higher education must battle with the ghost of the university past and expand its standard toolbox to empower new and established institutions to tailor their administrative structure and processes to better fulfill their campus purposes.

Notes

2. Why Does the New Campus Exist?

1. Michael Crow and William B. Dabars, *Designing the New American University* (Baltimore: Johns Hopkins University Press, 2015), 243.

3. Building a Campus with Purpose

1. Cathy N. Davidson, *The New Education: How to Revolutionize the University to Prepare Students for a World in Flux* (New York: Basic Books, 2017), 155.
2. Davidson, *The New Education*, 17–46.
3. Steven Johnson, *Where Good Ideas Come From: The Natural History of Innovation* (New York: Riverhead Books, 2010), 211–246.
4. I first heard the expression "exponential times" in the video titled "Did You Know" by Karl Frisch (https://www.youtube.com/watch?v =uo6BXgWbGvAfacts). I use this term repeatedly in the book to emphasize that the rate of change in accelerating. This catchphrase is often used in physics and engineering circles to denote that the rate of change is following an exponential function rather than a linear function. For an analysis of job growth and turnover in a technical report, see U.S. Department of Labor, Bureau of Labor Statistics, "Number of Jobs, Labor Market Experience, and Earnings Growth among Americans at 50: Results from a Longitudinal Survey," USDL-17-1158 (2017); World Economic Forum, "The Future of Jobs: Employment, Skills and Workforce Strategy for the Fourth Industrial

Revolution," Global Challenge Insight Report (January 2016), 1–167; and for an analysis and prediction of the expansion of new knowledge in a report on knowledge explosion, Marc Rosenberg, "Marc My Words: The Coming Knowledge Tsunami," October 10, 2017, https:// www.learningsolutionsmag.com/articles/2468/marc-my-words-the -coming-knowledge-tsunami

5. Joseph E. Aoun, *Robot-Proof Higher Education in the Age of Artificial Intelligence* (Cambridge, MA: MIT Press, 2017), ix–xxi.

6. Karl Frisch, "Did You Know," https://www.youtube.com/watch?v =uo6BXgWbGvA facts.

7. Clayton M. Christensen, *The Innovator's Dilemma: When New Technologies Cause Great Firms to Fail* (Harvard Business Review Press, 1997).

8. Clayton Christensen and Henry J. Eyring, *The Innovative University: Changing the DNA of Higher Education from the Inside Out* (John Wiley & Sons, 2011).

9. George Siemens, "New structures and spaces of learning: The systemic impact of connective knowledge, connectivism, and networked learning," (University of Manitoba, Presented for/to: Universidade do Minho Encontro sobre Web 2.0, Braga, Portugal, October 10, 2008). See discussion on p. 6.

10. Aoun, *Robot-Proof Higher Education*, xviii.

11. Davidson, *New Education*, 161.

12. There is discussion whether this quote can be directly attributed to Charles Darwin. See https://quoteinvestigator.com/2014/05/04/adapt/ for a discussion about the attribution of this quote.

13. W. Hobson and S. Rich, "Why Students Foot the Bill for College Sports, and How Some Are Fighting Back," *Washington Post*, November 13, 2015. Or see NCAA, "Finances of Intercollegiate Athletics," NCAA Report, http://www.ncaa.org/about/resources/research /finances-intercollegiate-athletics.

14. I learned about neural networks when I co-edited this book. W. Levy, J. Anderson, and S. Lehmkuhle, (eds.), *Synaptic Modification, Neuron Selectivity, and Nervous System Organization* (Mahwah, NJ: L. Erlbaum, 1985).

15. Benyamin B. Lichtenstein, Mary Uhl-Bien, Russ Marion, et al., "Complexity Leadership Theory: An Interactive Perspective on

Leading in Complex Adaptive Systems," *Emergence: Complexity and Organization* 8, no. 4 (2006): 2–12.

4. Structure with Purpose

1. William F. Massy. *Reengineering the University. How to Be Mission Centered, Market Smart, and Margin Conscious*, (Baltimore: Johns Hopkins University Press, 2016), 44.
2. Joseph E. Aoun, *Robot-Proof Higher Education in the Age of Artificial Intelligence*, (Cambridge, MA: MIT Press, 2017).
3. This list provides examples of the research conducted by UMR faculty. Many of these papers were products of UMR faculty working together. These published papers provide a snapshot of how a faculty redirected their disciplinary-based research skills and worked as interdisciplinary teams to study student learning and development.

Dame, L., Aryal, B., Huq, A., et al. "An Interdisciplinary Approach to Connecting Quantitative and Science Curricula and Pedagogy in an Undergraduate Program." *PRIMUS* 29, no. 8 (2018): 851–880. https://doi.org/10.1080/10511970.2018 .1532935.

Dingel, M. J., and Sage, S. "Dimensions of Difference, Sense of Belonging, and Fitting In: Tensions Around Developing Peer Groups, Student Body Diversity, and Academic Culture." *Learning Communities Journal* 8, no. 1 (2016): 131–156.

Dingel, Molly, and Wei, Wei. "Influences on Peer Evaluation: An Exploration of Leadership, Demographics, and Course Performance." *Assessment and Evaluation in Higher Education* 39, no. 6 (2014): 729–742. doi: 10.1080/02602938.2013.867477.

Dingel, Molly J., Wei, Wei, and Huq, Aminul. "Cooperative Learning and Peer Evaluation: The Effect of Free Riders on Team Performance and the Relationship Between Course Performance and Peer Evaluation." *Journal of Scholarship on Teaching and Learning* 13, no. 1 (2013): 45–56.

Dunbar, R. L. "Integrative Courses: Anatomy and Beyond." *Anatomical Sciences Education* 3, no. 2 (2010): 73–76.

Dunbar, R. L., Dingel, M. J., Dame, L. F., et al. "Student Social Self-Efficacy, Leadership Status, and Academic Performance in Collaborative Learning Environments." *Studies in Higher Education* 43, no. 9 (2018): 1507–1523. https://doi-org.ezp3.lib .umn.edu/10.1080/03075079.2016.1265496.

Dunbar, R. L., Dingel, M., and Prat-Resina, X. "Connecting Analytics and Curriculum Design: The Process and Outcome of Building a Tool to Browse Data Relevant to Course Designers." *Journal of Learning Analytics* 1, no. 3 (2014): 220–240.

Dunbar, R. L., and Nichols, M. D. "Fostering Empathy in Undergraduate Health Science Majors through the Reconciliation of Objectivity and Subjectivity: An Integrated Approach." *Anatomical Sciences Education* 5, no. 5 (May 4, 2012): 301–308. Epub.

Eklund, B. and Prat-Resina, X. "ChemEd X Data: Exposing Students to Open Scientific Data for Higher-Order Thinking and Self-Regulated Learning." *Journal of Chemical Education* 91, no. 9 (2014): 1501–1504.

Hsu, L., Heller, K., Xu, Q., et al. "Web-Based Problem-Solving Coaches for Physics Students." In "Cultivating Change in the Academy: 50+ Stories from the Digital Frontlines at the University of Minnesota in 2012," edited by A. H. Duin, E. Nater, and F. Anklesaria. University of Minnesota, University of Minnesota Digital Conservancy, http://purl.umn.edu/125273.

Huq, A., Hulsizer, H., and Wei, W. "Early Introduction of Hypothesis Testing In Introductory Statistics: A Pilot Study." *The Online Journal of New Horizons in Education* 8, no. 3 (2018), 10–19

Huq, A., Nichols, M. D., and Aryal, B. "Building Blocks: Threshold Concepts and Interdisciplinary Structures of Learning." In *Practice and Evidence of the Scholarship of Teaching and Learning*, (Rotterdam: Sense Publishing, 2016), 135–54.

Metzger, K. J. "Collaborative Teaching Practices in Undergraduate Active Learning Classrooms: A Report of Faculty Team Teaching Models and Student Reflections from Two Biology Courses." *Bioscene* 40, no. 1 (2015): 3–9.

Metzger, K. J. "Helping Students Conceptualize Species Divergence Events Using the Online Tool 'TimeTree: The Timescale of Life'." *American Biology Teacher* 73, no. 2 (2011): 106–108. http://www.jstor.org/stable/10.1525/abt.2011.73.2.9.

Metzger, K. J. "Starting right: Using 'Biophilia,' Organism Cards, and Key Themes in Biology to Introduce Student-Centered Active Learning Strategies at the Beginning of a Course." *American Biology Teacher* 75, no. 4 (2013): 285–289. http://www.jstor.org/stable/10.1525/abt.2013.75.4.11

Metzger, K. J, Montplaisir, D., Haines, D., et al., "Investigating Undergraduate Health Sciences Students' Acceptance of Evolution using MATE and GAENE." *Evolution: Education and Outreach* 11, no. 10 (2018): 1–18. https://doi.org/10.1186/s12052-018-0084-8.

Metzger, K. J. Smith, B. A., Brown, E., et al. "SMASH: A Diagnostic Tool to Monitor Student Metacognition, Affect, and Study Habits in an Undergraduate Science Course." *Journal of College Science Teaching* 47, no. 3 (2018): 91–99.

Metzger, K. J., and Yang Yowler, J. "Teaching mitosis and meiosis: Comparative effectiveness of two modeling approaches." *American Biology Teacher* 81, no. 2 (2019): 94–105.

Muthyala, R. S., and Wei, W. "Does Space Matter? Impact of Classroom Space on Student Learning in an Organic-First Curriculum." *Journal of Chemical Education* 90, no. 1 (2013): 45–50.

Nichols, M., Aryal, B., and Huq, A. "A Qualitative Case Study Exploring Student Comfort with Ambiguity in Physics, Math, and Literature." *Online Journal of New Horizons in Education* 8, no. 1 (2018).

Nichols, M. D., and Petzold, A. M. "Decrowning the Classroom King: Anatomy and Physiology and the Dangers of the Contact Zone." *Double Helix* 6, (2018): 1–15.

Peterson, M. T., Gruhlke, R. C., Sims, et al. "Blended Learning: Transformation of Phlebotomy Education at Mayo Clinic." *Clinical Laboratory Science* 29, no. 4 (2016): 219–226.

Petzold, A. M., and Dunbar, R. L. "The Art of Talking about Science: Beginning To Teach Physiology Students How To

Communicate with Nonscientists." *Advances in Physiology Education* 42, no. 2 (2018): 225–231. https://doi.org/10.1152/advan.00053.2017.

Petzold, A. M., Nicholas, M. D., and Dunbar, R. L. "Leveraging Creative Writing as a Tool for the Review of Foundational Physiological Content." *HAPS Educator* 20, no. 4 (2016): 76–84. doi: 10.21692/haps.2016.036.

Prat-Resina, X. "Using Data-Driven Activities with Chemed X Data To Practice Structure-Property Relationships in General Chemistry." *Chemistry Teacher International* 2018: 1–10. https://doi.org/10.1515/cti-2018-0010.

Smith, B., Metzger, K. J., and Soneral, P. "Research and Teaching: Investigation Introductory Nonmajor Biology Students' Self-Regulated Learning Strategies through the Implementation of a Reflective-Routine." *Journal of College Science Teaching* 48, no. 6 (2018). doi: 10.2505/4/jcst19_048_06_66.

Terrell, C. R., and Listenberger, L. L. "Using Molecular Visualization to Explore Protein Structure and Function and Enhance Student Facility with Computational Tools." *Biochemistry and Molecular Biology Education* 45, no. 4 (2017): 318–328. https://doi.org/10.1002/bmb.21040.

Wright, J. "In Defense of the Progressive Stack: A Strategy for Prioritizing Marginalized Voices During In-Class Discussion." *Teaching Philosophy* 41, no. 4 (2018): 407–428.

Wright, J. "Restricting Mobile Device Use in Introductory Philosophy Classrooms." *Teaching Philosophy* 39, no. 3 (2016): 307–327. doi: 10.5840/teachphil20168552.

Wright, J. "The Truth, but Not Yet: Avoiding Naïve Skepticism via Explicit Communication of Metadisciplinary Aims." *Teaching in Higher Education* 24, no. 3 (2019): 361–377. https://www.tandfonline.com/doi/pdf/10.1080/13562517.2018.1544552.

Wright-Peterson, V. "Making the Invisible Visible: Uncovering the Hidden Curriculum in Allied Health Education." In *The Hidden Curriculum in Health Professions Education*, edited by C. Bender, F. W., Hafferty, and J. O'Donnell (Hanover, NH: Dartmouth College Press).

4. Molly J. Dingel, Wei Wei, and Aminul Huq. "Cooperative Learning and Peer Evaluation: The Effect of Free Riders on Team Performance and the Relationship Between Course Performance and Peer Evaluation." *Journal of Scholarship on Teaching and Learning* 13, no. 1 (2013): 45–56.

5. R. L. Dunbar, M. J. Dingel, L. F. Dame, et al., "Student Social Self-Efficacy, Leadership Status and Academic Performance in Collaborative Learning Environments." *Studies in Higher Education* 43, no. 9 (2016): 1507–1523.

6. C. Neuhauser, and K. Weber. "The Student Success Coach." *New Directions for Higher Education* 2011, no. 153 (Spring 2011): 43–52.

7. "Wicked Problems" has become an expression to capture the complexity and the multiple interactions of societal problems. See https://en.wikipedia.org/wiki/Wicked_problem for a definition.

5. Buildings versus Space

1. For a discussion about the life cycle costs of a building, see Sieglinde Fuller, "Life-cycle cost analysis (LCCA)," (Washington, DC: Whole Building Design Guide, National Institute of Standards and Technology, 2016), https://www.wbdg.org/resources/life-cycle-cost-analysis-lcca.

2. For a discussion about calculating the costs of deferred maintenance, see, "$1 deferred maintenance = $4 needed later in capital . . . how does that math work?" *Dude Solutions* (blog) June 10, 2013, https://www.dudesolutions.com/community/discover/blogs/-1-deferred-maintenance-4-needed-later-in-capitalhow-does-that-math-work.

3. Lundy, Kasia, Ladd, Have, Gibbs, Roy, et al. "Public and Private Partnerships in Higher Education. What is Right for Your Institution?" Parthenon-EY Education practice. 2017: 1–16.

4. As examples of UMR public-private partnerships which conform to the planning principles, see 318 Commons video prepared by HGA, Stephen Lehmkuhle and Hal Henderson. https://www.youtube.com/watch?v=abA7azo3B-Y; and for Discovery Square, see "University of Minnesota Rochester Students Prepare to Learn Alongside Health Care Giants," *Destination Medical Center Newsletter*, September 4, 2019, issue 40, https://dmc.mn/university-of-minnesota-rochester-students-prepare-to-learn-alongside-healthcare-giants/.

6. Building and Flying the Plane at the Same Time

1. For articles about closing the achievement gap at UMR, see Mikhail Zinshteyn, "Achievement Gap Closed, One Chancellor Asks, 'Why Aren't We All Doing This?'," *The Hechinger Report*, Divided We Learn, June 27, 2019, https://hechingerreport.org/university-closes-its -achievement-gap/?utm_source=UMR+Campus+Distribution+List+ %28UMR+staff%2Cfaculty%2C+Nursing%2C+OT%2C+BICB%29& utm_campaign=513dc04c96-EMAIL_CAMPAIGN_2018_02_01 _COPY_01&utm_medium=email&utm_term=0_a5b91c1009 -513dc04c96-335878049. Also see G. Blumenstyk, and L. Gardner,. "A Health-Sciences Campus Focuses on Student Success," Innovation Imperative, *The Chronicle of Higher Education*, 2019, 36–37.

2. For a more recent expansion of the Peter Drucker quote, see Curt Coffman and Kathie Sorenson, *Culture Eats Strategy for Lunch* (Denver: Liang Addison Press, 2013).

7. What I Learned about Students and Faculty

1. Robert Zemsky, Gregory R. Wegner, and Ann J. Duffield, *Making Sense of the College Curriculum: Faculty Stories of Change, Conflict, and Accommodation* (New Brunswick, NJ: Rutgers University Press, 2018).

2. Robert Zemsky, *Checklist for Change: Making American Higher Education a Sustainable Enterprise* (New Brunswick, NJ: Rutgers University Press, 2013).

8. Leading by Purpose in Higher Education

1. Robert Zemsky, *Checklist for Change: Making American Higher Education a Sustainable Enterprise* (New Brunswick, NJ: Rutgers University Press, 2013), 115.

2. Robert Zemsky, Gregory R. Wegner, and Ann J. Duffield, *Making Sense of the College Curriculum: Faculty Stories of Change, Conflict, and Accommodation* (New Brunswick, NJ: Rutgers University Press, 2018).

3. Robert Zemsky, *Making Reform Work: The Case for Transforming American Higher Education* (New Brunswick, NJ: Rutgers University Press, 2009).

4. William Massy, *Economics of Education. Resource Allocation in Higher Education* (Ann Arbor, MI: The University of Michigan Press, 1996).

5. See "The Delaware Cost Study: The National Study of Instructional Costs and Productivity," University of Delaware, 2016, https://ire.udel .edu/cost/.

6. See "Finances of Intercollegiate Athletics," NCAA Report, 2018, http://www.ncaa.org/about/resources/research/finances-intercollegiate -athletics.

7. See W. Hobson and S. Rich, "Why Students Foot the Bill for College Sports, and How Some Are Fighting Back," *Washington Post*, November 13, 2015.

Epilogue

1. See the discussion of micro-models in chapter 7 in Robert Zemsky, *Checklist for Change: Making American Higher Education a Sustainable Enterprise* (New Brunswick, NJ: Rutgers University Press, 2013), 123–125.

Index

campus purpose (cont.)

knowledge hierarchy, 34

leaders: change, 3, 14; custodial, 3, 11, 13, 29; demands on in adaptive organizations, 46–47
leadership: change, 7, 10–12; complex/collaborative, 47
learning: knowing and becoming and, 38–39, 96–97; rapid rate of change and changing definition of, 35
learning-design faculty (tenure-track) at UMR, 54, 56, 103, 105
Learning Labs (classrooms), 71
learning object, 65–66
learning outcomes: learning objects and, 65–67; measurable, 24–25
legacy, mission and, x, xi
"Leverage Our Place," 22
liability risk of intercollegiate athletics, 121–122, 123, 124
Lichtenstein, Benyamin B., 47
listening tour, 14–17; university staff and, 29
literacies for new artificial intelligence world, 57

majors, 60; in health professions, 67; in health sciences, 67
Making Sense of the College Curriculum (Zemsky, Wegner & Duffield), 105
market forces driving change in new institutions, 130–131, 132
mascot, UMR, 42–43
Massive Open Online Courses (MOOCs), 37
Massy, William, 50
Mayo Clinic: Center for Innovation at, 80; as major employer in Rochester, 8; sleep clinic, 101; students interacting with leaders of, 10; student volunteers at, 22, 80–81; UMR adding value to Rochester community and, 20; UMR partnership with, 15, 22, 68

Mayo Clinic leaders, author's listening tour and, 14–15
Mayo Clinic School of Health Sciences, bachelor of science offering in collaboration with, 68
measuring learning outcomes, 24–25
media, intercollegiate athletics and, 121
medical school, UMR graduates attending, 69
mental energy, managing, 39–40; faculty, 54; student success coaches, 76
mission statements, x–xi, 108
music by the bedside, 80–81

nanotechnology, as suggested programmatic area for UMR, 5, 15
networks: grounding values and centering aspirations and leveraging, 95; pedagogy and, 71; power of, 44–45, 71; properties of, 45–46, 47
Neuhauser, Claudia, 65
new campus: assumptions about, 130; focus on people, 130; innovation and, 130, 131–132
New Education, The (Davidson), 28, 30
New Faculty Teaching Scholars (University of Missouri), 50–51
new knowledge: creation and dissemination of, 34–35; exponential growth of, 35–36
nontenure track faculty policies, 51

online learning, 37
open source education and research networks, 34
organizational chart, purposes and, 108–109
organizational structures, academic disciplines and, 109–110
out-of-the-classroom experiences, 22–23

parents, skepticism about UMR curriculum, 62–63
passion, resilience and students', 101–102

About the Author

STEPHEN LEHMKUHLE was the inaugural chancellor for the University of Minnesota Rochester from 2007 to 2017. Prior to 2007, he served for a decade as vice president for academic affairs at the University of Missouri. Dr. Lehmkuhle has published widely in visual neuroscience.

Made in United States
North Haven, CT
14 November 2021